The History of

DINERS

in New Jersey

The History of DINERS in *New Jersey*

MICHAEL C. GABRIELE

AMERICAN PALATE

Published by American Palate
A Division of The History Press
Charleston, SC 29403
www.historypress.net

Cover: Front image of Curzon's Diner, Paterson, courtesy of Bob Hazekamp, Passaic County Historical Society, Paterson. Back photo of Key City Diner sign, Phillipsburg, by author.

First published 2013

Manufactured in the United States

ISBN 978.1.60949.822.1

Library of Congress CIP data applied for.

Notice: The information in this book is true and complete to the best of our knowledge. It is offered without guarantee on the part of the author or The History Press. The author and The History Press disclaim all liability in connection with the use of this book.

Nighthawks at the diner
Of Emma's 49er
There's a rendezvous of strangers
Around the coffee urn tonight
All the gypsy hacks, the insomniacs
Now the paper's been read
Now the waitress said:
"Eggs and sausage and a side of toast
Coffee and a roll
Hash browns over easy
Chili in a bowl
With burgers and fries
What kind of pie?"

—"Eggs And Sausage (in a Cadillac with Susan Michelson),"
written by Tom Waits, from the 1975 album Nighthawks at the Diner,
released on Asylum Records

Sunday brunch, Mustache Bill's Diner, Barnegat Light, Long Beach Island, July 2012. *Photo by M. Gabriele.*

Contents

Acknowledgements

I'd like to thank The History Press, especially Dani McGrath and Whitney Tarella Landis, for giving me the opportunity to write this book.

There are numerous people to thank for their support in this project. The list includes Barbara McGeary Marhoefer, Richard J.S. Gutman, Larry Cultrera, Marilyn Kelly Lamoreau and Joyce Kelly Stanford, Eileen and Peter Glenn, Don and Newly Preziosi, John Baeder, Michael Aaron Rockland, Mark S. Auerbach, Les Cooper, Randy Garbin, Steve Harwin, Donald E. Prout, Claire Trudgen Dixon, Gregory Ramoundos, Dr. George E. Antoniou, John E. Sakellaris, Patricia Klindienst, Anthony Natale, Mary Corcodilos, Frances Fazio, Joe Fazio, Erwin C. Fedkenheuer, Elaine Swingle and family, Frank Conte, Herbert Enyart, Robert Kullman, Harold Kullman, Mary Quinn, John Hallanan, Joseph Ryan, Stephanie L. Cherry-Farmer, Patrick Reilly, William Davey, Melissa McNally, Reverend Monsignor Francis R. Seymour, Kathy Grimshaw, Tom Ankner, Nicholas James Van Dorn, Kathryn Staropoli, Thomas Beisler, Andrew Hurley, Carole Bosko, Karen Kilpatrick, Mark Mariano, Bill Leaver, Vinnie Altier, Joan Hart, Kim Luke, Gail Scovell, Paul L. Eichlin, Heather Schaefer, Barbara Jensen, Bob Hazekamp, Carol Magazino, Deborah Davies, Jim Van Lenten, Bill Schelling, Carol H. McNeil, Peter Genovese and Mark McEachern.

This book is dedicated to all my sources—those mentioned here and many others—the kind, generous, thoughtful people who shared information, images and memories. Their assistance is greatly appreciated.

Note from the author: All towns and cities mentioned in the text are located in New Jersey unless otherwise indicated.

The Isosceles Trapezoid

A light rain was falling in Nutley on August 17, 1977. That afternoon, a crowd of forty people gathered near the intersection of Franklin Avenue and Centre Street to watch the end of the Franklin Diner.

Passersby who congregated on that overcast afternoon held umbrellas, stood quietly and saw the dismantling of the diner unfold. This author, working at the time as a staff writer for the *Nutley Sun*, the weekly town newspaper, covered the event. In the August 25, 1977 edition of the *Sun*, I reported that the diner was removed to make room for a three-store complex and parking lot.

Prior to the start of the demolition, I had a chance to talk with the construction crew and take a quick look inside the diner, which was shuttered in September 1976. "Isn't this some kind of a landmark or something?" one of the workers asked as he opened the door for me. Beneath the dust and grime that had accumulated over the one-year period when the diner was out of service, the Nutley eatery had well-preserved wooden walls, glass-brick appointments, booths, stools and a marble countertop. There were multiple panes of colorful "milk" glass built into slots on the diner's front wall as an architectural accent. An autographed photo of Roosevelt "Rosey" Brown, a National Football League Hall of Fame offensive tackle who played for the New York Giants, hung over the grill.

Ronald Koch assumed ownership of the diner in 1973 from his father and uncle, Hugo and Oscar Koch, who were the proprietors since the late 1930s. There was a Franklin Diner at the site as far back as the early 1930s.

Franklin Diner, Nutley. *Courtesy of Richard J.S. Gutman.*

An ad posted in the July 7, 1933 edition of the *Sun* announced that the Franklin Diner was "completely renovated" and had opened under the "new management" of E.H. Sutherland.

Nutley was losing a beloved, albeit unkempt, landmark. Some residents, including then mayor Harry Chenoweth, nostalgically recounted the diner's place in town lore. It was, he said, a popular social and political haunt. The mayor recalled that Commissioner Francis T. Stager was "practically elected at the diner." The Franklin Diner ran a twenty-four-hour business until November 22, 1963—the fateful day when President John F. Kennedy was assassinated. An early-morning fire caused significant damage to the premises. Following the accident, all-night service was discontinued.

Demolition work began at 12:30 p.m. Using a twenty-five-ton crane and other equipment, V. Ottilio and Sons of Paterson removed the diner—a job that took four hours. The crane operator was a man named "Sonny." The modular structure rested on a steel I-beam foundation. The crane first tore off the roof and then systematically dislodged sections of the exterior walls.

Located at 397 Centre Street, the Franklin was an O'Mahony diner. Jerry O'Mahony was a premier builder of golden-age diners. Today, relatively few O'Mahony diner cars survive. The demise of the Franklin Diner, a tale more than thirty-five years old, chronicles a single event for one town and a particular diner. However, it does contain elements of a larger story—the challenges associated with the survival of vintage diners in the Garden State and the colorful history they embody. In the run-up to the demolition, the June 9, 1977 edition of the *Nutley Sun* reported that there were discussions on possible options to save the diner or move it to another location, none of which panned out.

NEW JERSEY IS the "Diner Capital of America," a title rightfully bestowed on the Garden State by various publications. *New Jersey Monthly*, in a cover story in its October 1977 edition, issued this proclamation. An April 29, 1984 feature in the *Star-Ledger* declared that New Jersey was "unrivaled as the diner capital of the Western world." Numerous articles over the years in the *New York Times* have sung the praises of Garden State diners. The title refers to the vast number of diners that populate the state, as well as how diners, during the last one hundred years, have become a distinct part of New Jersey's roadside culture.

The title also is a tribute to the many diner builders that once were based in New Jersey—a cluster of independent companies, now virtually extinct, that skillfully created these architectural gems. The Garden State was the factory that produced diners in the twentieth century. These were sophisticated manufacturers that utilized advanced design and engineering techniques, pioneered the concept of modular construction and mastered the use of leading-edge industrial materials.

Diners have inspired paintings, books, music videos and movies; kindled reunions and romances; and served as oases for hungry travelers. Randy Garbin, who has written several books on diners and is the founder of the website www.roadsideonline.com, estimated that there are 370 diners in the Garden State that he identifies as "true, prefabricated" eateries and not "storefront properties" or "site-built" restaurants.

On that dreary Wednesday afternoon in August 1977, after watching the Franklin Diner come down, I stashed my notebook and packed up my camera. The demolition audience dispersed. The rain tapered off, but the sky remained cloudy and dark—a brooding backdrop for the day's events. As I was leaving the scene, the demolition worker who earlier had opened the door to the diner signaled to me. He held an intact section of the decorative

Photo by M. Gabriele.

milk glass, in the shape of an isosceles trapezoid, which had been located above each of the diner windows. Somehow, as the structure was being torn apart, the delicate glass pane miraculously had survived the drama.

"Here. This is for you," he said, handing me the milk glass. "Keep it." I thanked him, and with a knowing smile, he turned and walked away to finish his work.

The pane of milk glass was all that was left of the place where Commissioner Stager was "practically elected," that was damaged by fire on the day JFK was killed, that had an autographed photo of Rosey Brown hanging over the grill and that was owned by two guys named Hugo and Oscar.

What happened to the isosceles trapezoid? I've kept it all these years. Here it is.

Part I

In Our Line, We Lead the World

THE BAYONNE WAGON BUILDER

July 3, 1912, marks the start of New Jersey's diner history. On this date, a man named Michael J. Griffin purchased a lunch wagon—the horse-drawn precursor to modern diners—for $800 from Jerry O'Mahony. Jerry, with the help of his younger brother, Daniel, built the wagon in the backyard of Jerry's Bayonne home, which was located at 7 East Sixteenth Street. O'Mahony was the grand innovator of the modern American diner.

Barbara McGeary Marhoefer, a granddaughter of Jerry O'Mahony and company archivist, provided a copy of the first contract, which was signed by Griffin. The document specified that the "lunch cart" would be situated at the intersection of Paterson Plank Road, Summit Avenue and DeMott Street in West Hoboken, which today is an area of Union City. At the time, this intersection was known as "Transfer Station," which was the confluence of several trolley lines in downtown West Hoboken, according to Internet postings.

There were other builders of lunch wagons outside New Jersey before the launch of the O'Mahony operations in Bayonne. The Patrick J. Tierney Company of New Rochelle, New York, was one, and the T.H. Buckley Car Manufacturing Company and the Worcester Lunch Car and Carriage Manufacturing Company, both of Worcester, Massachusetts, were also leading builders of lunch wagons before O'Mahony's entry into the market.

A CONTRACT.

Received of Daniel A. Mahoney, of the City of Bayonne, County of Hudson, State of New Jersey, one Lunch Cart situate at the corner of Paterson Plank Road, Summit Avenue and DeMott Street, West Hoboken, New Jersey, for which I agree to pay to him the sum of Eight Hundred ($800) Dollars in manner following, to wit.- One Hundred ($100) Dollars upon the date hereof, and Ten ($10) Dollars each and every week until the whole amount is paid, with the weekly payments to be paid on Monday of each week, together with interest at the rate of 6% per annum from the date hereof; on all sums remaining unpaid interest to be paid weekly at the time of paying the weekly instalment.

Said Lunch Cart is to be and remain the sole and absolute property of said Daniel A. Mahoney until the whole of such sum and interest is paid, and I agree that I will keep said property insured in favor of said Daniel A. Mahoney against loss by fire for a sum not less than Eight Hundred ($800) Dollars, and I will keep said property in good condition and repair, and I will be absolutely responsible for the same; and I will pay said sum and interest notwithstanding any injury to the total destruction of the property from any cause whatsoever, deducting, however, net amount which said Daniel A. Mahoney may receive from insurance made as above. Upon the payment of the whole of said sum and interest as above set forth, said property is to become mine, but upon default upon my part in payment of any of the above instalments, including interest the whole unpaid balance shall thereupon be due and payable and said Daniel A. Mahoney shall have a right to take the property at once into his possession, and unless the total amount remaining unpaid, including interest, expenses of taking possession of and keeping the property and other lawful charges, is paid within five (5) days from such default, all my right to purchase said property shall cease, and said Daniel A. Mahoney shall have the right to retain all sums paid in this agreement as compensation for the use of such property while in my possession.

This contract is executed and delivered at Bayonne, N. J. The cart is taken possession of by me at West Hoboken, and all payments are to be made by order of said Daniel A. Mahoney. If I should fail to keep and perform the terms and conditions of this contract, I agree to return the cart to Daniel A. Mahoney at Bayonne.

WITNESS MY HAND THIS *Third* DAY OF

JULY, NINETEEN TWELVE.

Michael Griffin

IN PRESENCE OF

jeremiah Mahony

First O'Mahony lunch wagon contract, signed by Michael Griffin. *Courtesy of Barbara McGeary Marhoefer.*

All were cashing in on the popular "night-lunch" business, an after-hours pit stop for workingmen. In addition, New Jersey's Paterson Wagon Company, later to be known as the Paterson Vehicle Company, was manufacturing a wide range of horse-drawn, customized carriages and wagons for farmers, merchants and municipal use, such as for police and fire departments. It's plausible that lunch wagons were included in those production efforts.

Richard J.S. Gutman's 1979 book *American Diner*, the first history of the diner industry ever published, laid the foundation for the study of this field of Americana. Gutman traced the humble beginnings of lunch wagons and the "night-lunch" business to Westminster Street in Providence, Rhode Island, in 1872 and to a horse-drawn wagon owned by Walter Scott, who sold sandwiches, boiled eggs, pies and coffee to passersby. Gutman explained that the night-lunch business was born out of necessity. "Nighthawks, late-night workers, and carousers couldn't get anything to eat anywhere [in Providence] after 8 p.m., when all the restaurants closed for the evening," he wrote. On the other hand, Gutman wrote that lunch wagons also served the needs of a more mainstream clientele, providing "a milieu that was comfortable for the working-class people who ate there."

The June 19, 1948 edition of the *Saturday Evening Post*, in an article titled "The Diner Puts on Airs," profiled a man named Eddie Conlon of North Bergen, who opened his "first" wagon in 1904. "His place seated seven

Palace Café, Rahway, circa 1908. *Courtesy of Don and Newly Preziosi.*

customers and could be moved by borrowing a horse somewhere. He carried water for coffee in a pail from the nearest house and clambered to the roof [of the wagon] every night to fill the gasoline tank, which fed fuel to his stove."

The O'Mahony/Griffin transaction is the beginning of the Garden State's diner history, as it documents a lunch wagon built and bought by Jersey guys. Bayonne and Union City are the hallowed grounds for the origin of New Jersey's diner business. After purchasing his first wagon, Griffin signed a second contract on October 23, 1912, for another O'Mahony wagon for a price of $1,000. This lunch wagon was delivered to the Blaney/Spooner property on Summit Avenue in Jersey City. Blaney/Spooner was the site of the Orpheum Theater, located at 597 Summit Avenue at the corner of Cottage Street, in a neighborhood known as "Five Corners." The theater was opened in 1910 near the old Hudson/Manhattan subway station (today's Journal Square). The 1918 Jersey City Directory lists Michael J. Griffin as a restaurant owner; however, there is no listing for him in either the 1915 or 1922 directories, suggesting that his lunch wagon business was short-lived. The Orpheum Theater was torn down in the early 1960s, and the site today is a parking lot.

"Jerry O'Mahony was a pivotal figure in the diner manufacturing business," Gutman, the director and curator of the Culinary Arts Museum at Johnson & Wales University in Providence, Rhode Island, said during a July 2012 interview. "O'Mahony diners became the standard by which all others were judged. His company built fabulous diners. They were stylish—not too outrageous, not too conservative." An unsung entrepreneur in New Jersey's business history, O'Mahony had the vision, confidence and determination "to lead the world in his line," Gutman said, quoting the phrase that served as the O'Mahony marketing slogan ("In our line, we lead the world"). "His contributions were amazingly important in the history of diners. These were iconic buildings that he and other diner builders created."

Opposite, top: This photo, taken on July 4, 1918, shows the Land & Bassing "quick lunch" wagon at 1 Central Avenue in downtown Passaic. The crowd had gathered to watch a parade of World War I soldiers, an event that was held in honor of a visit by President Theodore Roosevelt. The lunch wagon was adjacent to the Passaic station on the Main Line of the Erie Railroad in the heart of the downtown area. *Courtesy of Mark S. Auerbach, Passaic city historian.*

Opposite, bottom: Trenton Inter-State Fair, the Capitol lunch wagon, circa 1905. *Courtesy of Don and Newly Preziosi.*

Eating on Wheels

The December 1921 edition of the *American Restaurant* magazine featured an article penned by O'Mahony titled "Eating on Wheels," which described lunch wagons. The thrust of the story focused on how the lunch wagon was a flexible, efficient way to deliver quality food to customers. "As a means of purveying food to the public, the lunch car has no equal…no type of hotel or restaurant can compete with it from an economic standpoint. One competent lunch man can serve promptly and satisfactorily twice the number of people that two men can manage in a restaurant." He wrote that the lunch wagon's wheels gave the proprietor the advantage of relocating to various locations to better serve customers. "Think of that in comparison with the owner of a building, who would have to sell his property before he could change his location."

O'Mahony also provided details of his wagons:

> In the construction of our cars, we use the best material and build each car to meet the build-code requirements of the locality in which they are to be operated. Our car is all tile and quartered oak, interior finish furnished with skylights, screens and steps and mounted on a heavy running gear. Equipped with a combination set of three, four-gallon coffee urns, one eight-inset steam table, one four-burner with griddle attached short order cooker, one double oven range, three German silver hoods, one exhaust fan and rheostat, two ceiling fans, one tiled interior refrigerator, cutting boards, pie racks, closets and drawers…systems for hot and cold water, gas and electricity…countertop marble and all-white enamel stools with foot rail brackets attached.

An article in the June 1922 edition of *Printers Ink Monthly*, "Selling Restaurants on Wheels," described the origins of O'Mahony's diner manufacturing business, noting that O'Mahony "ten years ago, was interested in watching old-fashioned lunch cars in his home town of Bayonne." However, O'Mahony was doing far more than just watching. As a young man, he ran a bar in Bayonne and no doubt used that experience as a benchmark to study and compare the subtle points of the lunch wagon business. In a 1996 self-published booklet, *Jerry O'Mahony: Dining Car Pioneer*, Marhoefer wrote that O'Mahony, around the year 1908, was sold on the concept of lunch wagons. He bought one and opened it for business with his brother, Daniel. The wagon did so well that they expanded to a larger model

Photo of an O'Mahony lunch wagon interior. *Courtesy of Barbara McGeary Marhoefer.*

and "soon owned and operated seven of them." Based on their success, the brothers decided that it would be profitable to build their own wagons.

The November 18, 1922 edition of *Collier's* magazine reported that "Jerry O'Mahony is known as the largest manufacturer of lunch wagons in the world. Ten years ago he saw his chance to specialize. He built and sold two small wagons that year [to Griffin]. This year it will be forty."

Marhoefer described a lunch wagon as a small, mobile eatery, towed by horses to choice locations for business, such as outside a factory or near a train station. Lunch wagons had small kitchens "where a cook served people at an inside counter and also took orders through an open window," she wrote. Marhoefer noted that people enjoyed the intimate experience of sitting inside the small confines of the wagon and watching as the grill man prepared food. The customers' close-up encounter with the cooking process—all its appealing sights, sounds and smells—was part of the lunch wagon's allure.

The O'Mahony 1922 sales brochure advised diner owners to serve hamburgers, ham, bacon, steaks, frankfurters, roast beef, loin pork, goulash, lamb stew, potatoes, onions and canned goods. "This was franchising years before McDonald's," Marhoefer said. "Lunch wagons specialized in serving simple, hearty food—quickly and inexpensively." She cited items on a menu board from a wagon built in the late teens, the Crescent Lunch. The selections included steak and potatoes (twenty-five cents); liver and bacon, liver and onions or hamburger steak (twenty cents, including potatoes); ham, eggs and potatoes (twenty cents); two eggs any style (fifteen cents); ham and beans (fifteen cents); hamburgers (ten cents); ham and egg sandwich (ten cents); Klondike sandwiches (salted herring, ten cents); and pie or cake (five cents per slice).

Life on the Peninsula

Jerry (Jeremiah) O'Mahony was born in Bayonne on October 1, 1880. He and his wife, Kate, along with their first child, Catherine Teresa, resided on East Sixteenth Street. Marhoefer, the daughter of Catherine Teresa, recalling family anecdotes, said that young Jerry worked for a man who sold hot dogs and cold drinks, transported by a cart, at baseball games in Bayonne. Joseph Ryan, Bayonne city historian and public information officer, said that baseball was played at several Bayonne locations during the 1890s. For example, Ryan cited the book *Images of America: Bayonne* by Kathleen M. Middleton, who identified a ball field near Newark Bay, opposite Fourth Street, that was owned by the New Jersey Athletic Club.

Bayonne, which became a township in 1861, was a vibrant port and the perfect environment to support Jerry O'Mahony's ambitions in the diner business. Ryan said that Bayonne was a gateway for the southern and eastern European immigrants arriving in the early twentieth century. Following World War I, Bayonne had a rush of immigration, and the city's population soared to eighty-eight thousand people (by way of comparison, when O'Mahony was born in 1880, Bayonne's population was only nine thousand).

The timing of this rapid growth coincided with the rise of O'Mahony's lunch wagon business. For O'Mahony's manufacturing operations, these European immigrants distinguished themselves as a skilled labor force for working with materials that went into diners: wood, metal, marble, glass, terrazzo floors and ceramic tile. Ryan said that the immigrants also became working-class diner customers who found employment in Bayonne's extensive oil refineries and petrochemical business sector—eating out at Bayonne diners on their lunch breaks and after work. By 1915, Bayonne's major industries included Standard Oil, the big industrial employer of this

Jerry O'Mahony and family. *Courtesy of Barbara McGeary Marhoefer.*

era; Babcock & Wilcox (metalworking); Edible Products Company (refined cottonseed oil); International Nickel Company; Safety Insulated Wire & Cable Company/General Cable; and Schwarzenbach-Huber Silk Goods. As for logistical support, Bayonne had several waterfront facilities for transporting O'Mahony diners.

Bayonne waterfront, circa 1922. An O'Mahony diner (Jack's Tile Lunch) is being loaded onto a river barge. *Courtesy of Barbara McGeary Marhoefer.*

Following the initial sales to Michael Griffin, O'Mahony built a lunch wagon for a partnership known as Kelly and Bivens. May 5, 1913, was the date of this contract, with a purchase price of $1,900. Following this transaction, there were twenty-one additional wagons sold during the next three years. By 1916, the cost for an O'Mahony wagon had climbed to $4,200.

The 1914–15 edition of the Bayonne City Directory listed Jerry O'Mahony as a wagon manufacturer. On April 28, 1917, the lunch wagon manufacturing business in Bayonne was incorporated under the name Jerry O'Mahony Inc., with the company's address listed at 49 Lexington Avenue. Jerry O'Mahony received 450 shares of stock, while John J. Hanf—a carpenter, family friend and now a business partner—got 49 shares (with 1 share going to Hanf's wife, Agnes). Jerry's brother, Daniel, following the 1912 sale of wagons to Griffin, was no longer involved in the wagon business but rather operated his own restaurants.

One year after incorporating, O'Mahony built a lunch car and brought it to New York City, at a spot on Seventh Avenue and Thirty-fourth Street,

24

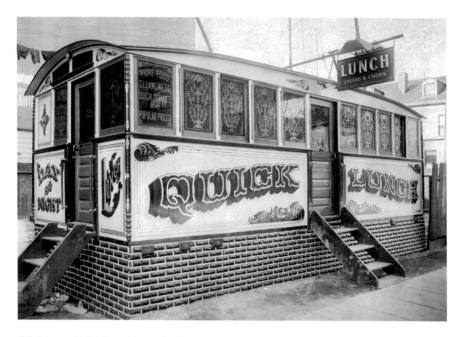

O'Mahony Quick Lunch car; sign in window reads, "Pure food, cleanliness, quick service and popular prices." *Courtesy of Barbara McGeary Marhoefer.*

dubbing it the Walkor Lunch. Sparked by the success of this venture, he built and ran other Walkor lunch cars and developed a chain, which was incorporated in 1916. He also established another business unit, Club Diners Inc. (incorporated in the state of Delaware in 1926), which also managed lunch cars. A third line followed, known as JOM Lunch. "Jerry's own diner businesses helped provide the first-hand knowledge he needed to keep redesigning new models to make them better," Marhoefer wrote.

Early lunch wagons built by O'Mahony were barrel-roofed models. Custom designs were available, but the standard size was ten feet wide by twenty-six feet long. The cars were elaborately painted and decorated. Citing information from the 1922 company brochure, Marhoefer wrote that "Jerry was filled with a vision of bigger things. He visualized a deluxe car as a complete restaurant, containing every modern convenience." According to Marhoefer, part of his inspiration came from the well-appointed Pullman "Palace" railroad cars of the era, which were the gold standard for industrial craftsmanship.

The evolution from a compact, mobile, horse-drawn lunch cart to a larger diner car at a fixed location was a major shift, and O'Mahony was a central figure in this transformation. Gutman noted that the early generations of diners coincided with the post–World War I boom throughout the United States. In terms of the new design concepts, diner form followed function as the customer base took shape and grew. "Diners at this time had much more equipment, in addition to a lot more storage and work space," Gutman wrote. "There were steam tables, burners, griddles, iceboxes and sandwich boards. Now there were dishes, bowls, and mugs to store and wash, along with pots and pans and utensils."

Location, Location, Location

In 1932, the O'Mahony Company conducted a survey of its customers, which revealed that most had no previous experience in the diner business. They were bus drivers, bond brokers, clerks, college professors, bookkeepers, salesmen, housewives and gas station attendants. As a result, these novice entrepreneurs relied on the diner builder for business advice. "In the early days, diner owners and diner builders maintained a close, professional relationship," Gutman said. "O'Mahony understood how important this was. He and the other diner builders wanted the diner operators to succeed [so they could buy more diners]." O'Mahony realized that in addition to building high-quality lunch wagons, he also had to provide an array of services to support diner owners. This included guidance on developing a menu, picking food vendors, designing kitchens, training employees and selecting a promising site to conduct business. O'Mahony weighed many variables to match a prospective diner owner with a choice location and went to great lengths to be sure it was a good fit.

Location was the primary topic of conversation in the spring of 1927 when O'Mahony arranged a meeting in Hightstown between Benjamin Zaitz, a landowner and dairy farmer, and the Corcodilos family. Nicholas A. Corcodilos owned the Presto Restaurant in Perth Amboy but was dissatisfied with the tempo of life in the port city and wanted to move his family to more rural surroundings. Born on the Greek island of Andros, Corcodilos attended a culinary school while growing up in Greece and came to America in the early 1900s. He demonstrated his superior cooking skills and landed jobs at hotels in Boston and Saint Augustine, Florida, later finding work as a chef at Columbia University before moving to Perth Amboy.

He was introduced to O'Mahony through a mutual business associate. O'Mahony—aware of Corcodilos's desire for a change of scenery—discussed the opportunity to open a lunch wagon in Hightstown. It was virgin territory, and even though the area was dominated by farmland, the site he had spotted (property owned by Zaitz at the corner of Mercer and Ward Streets) was located on a roadway (old Route 33) that connected Philadelphia and New York and was near the town's train station. O'Mahony's instincts told him that this spot had the potential to support a lunch wagon.

Corcodilos—along with his wife, Asimina; sons, Anthony and Jim; and six-year-old daughter, Mary—boarded a train in Perth Amboy on a beautiful Sunday morning and traveled to the farmlands of Hightstown. Zaitz and O'Mahony met the Corcodilos family at the Hightstown train station and provided a tour of the area. Mary, interviewed in 2012, said that her father immediately was impressed "and thanked God that his dream was becoming a reality. Before the day was over he had negotiated a deal with both gentlemen. Land was bought and contracts were signed. No lawyer was involved." The price was $7,000, a sum Corcodilos could afford after selling his home and restaurant in Perth Amboy. In addition to the lunch wagon and property, the transaction included an existing building on the site, which was renovated to serve as the family home. Within six months, a lunch wagon was built and transported by truck to Hightstown. There was, however, a tragic note in the story. Mary said that her mom died shortly after the train ride to Hightstown, leaving her dad to carry on alone.

On moving day, Mary said that the family piled into their Pontiac, met an O'Mahony truck in Edison and followed it to Hightstown. She noted that the lunch wagon was "cute," with canvas awnings over the windows and hand-painted lettering and designs on the exterior walls. The Hightstown Diner was open for business. "Mr. O'Mahony was a wonderful man," Mary Corcodilos recalled. "Even though I was a little girl, I remember him very well. He knew all about the lunch wagon business and always wanted to help people. After my father started the business, Mr. O'Mahony came to visit us several times. He gave my father advice and answered any questions that my father had." As part of the deal, Corcodilos negotiated to get fresh milk from Zaitz's dairy farm, which he used to make homemade butter and cream.

Mary shared another vivid memory: the lunch wagon in Hightstown had an unspoken but clearly understood men-only policy. "Only men waiters and cooks and only men customers, who consisted of farmers, traders and local business men," frequented the Hightstown wagon, Mary wrote. "Women were not to be seen in a lunch wagon. I had to stand outside the door to get my ice cream cone, while my brothers ate theirs at the counter." This attitude prevailed throughout the diner business during this period, according to Marhoefer. She wrote that women didn't go to most diners "because they were uncomfortable sitting at counters," due to the social mores and stereotypes that existed. But by the early 1930s, the discriminatory practices against women had eased, and more enlightened minds prevailed. O'Mahony and other diner builders began to include signs on their eateries that declared "ladies invited" and noted that "table service" was available.

Vivian and Clarence

In the early days of the twentieth century, three ambitious young men from the Catskill region of New York State traveled to New Jersey. Two friends from Hardenburgh, New York—Vivian Wilbur Kelly and George Millard Knapp—along with their chum Clarence Bivens, from nearby Lew Beach, were hoping to find jobs. It was the thing that many young men from that neck of the woods did during this period: leave the rustic farming villages to find work and another way of life.

As mentioned, Kelly and Bivens purchased an O'Mahony lunch wagon on May 5, 1913. Much like the spot selected by Michael Griffin for his lunch wagons, Kelly and Bivens chose a strategic location for their wagon that involved proximity to mass transit. Their wagon was situated near the intersection of Midland Avenue and Elm Street in downtown Arlington (today a section of Kearny)—adjacent to the plaza of the Arlington train station, Depot Square, which was a stop on the old Greenwood Lake/Erie Railway. The train line, with a terminus in Hoboken, was used by commuters and, prior to the 1920s, transported ice commercially harvested during the winter months from Greenwood Lake, New York, to New York City merchants and warehouses. In addition, Elm Street had a trolley car line, so the two modes of rail transportation provided the partners with a steady, profitable stream of customers most hours of the day.

The 1915 Kearny City Directory listed Kelly and Bivens as the owners of the lunch wagon at 170 Midland Avenue. In addition to being near the rail line and trolley, the wagon was in a business district (downtown Arlington at the time). The neighborhood had a bakery, a butcher shop, a newspaper office, a hotel and a pharmacy, as well as a nearby dairy in Kearny. Today, only steel and concrete vestiges of the Arlington station remain in the

Postcard of Depot Square, Arlington train station, dated 1912. Note the trolley car traveling on Elm Street in the center of the photo. *Courtesy of Sandra McCleaster.*

residential Kearny neighborhood, along with sections of the track and rusted signal equipment. Train service on the Greenwood Lake line ended in 1966, and trolley service ceased in the 1940s.

Re-creating a typical daily schedule from 1913, Gutman said that each morning, the two partners would have received deliveries of fresh meat, vegetables, bread, pie, milk, cream and eggs. Much like today's diners, breakfast was available at any hour of the day. Why? "Everyone loves breakfast," Gutman explained. "It's comfort food." The lunch wagon's daily menu included stews, soups, sandwiches, ham and beans, an assortment of egg platters and coffee. The compact wagon interior had stools alongside a marble countertop for customers (no booths), along with a grill, a steam table, an oven, a stove and a small icebox.

Before buying the O'Mahony wagon, Kelly and Knapp operated the Hudson Café, a lunch wagon located on the Belleville Turnpike in Kearny, circa 1909. Eileen Glenn, Clarence's granddaughter, said that the T.H. Buckley Company built the Hudson Café wagon. At some point between the closing of the Hudson Café and the opening of Kelly and Bivens's O'Mahony lunch wagon in 1913, George Millard Knapp left the scene, returning to Hardenburgh.

Bivens, in a newspaper article that announced his October 9, 1912 marriage to Mary Ann Colclough (pronounced "Coakley"), stated he was also the proprietor of Chelsea Lunch in Harrison. The marriage certificate lists Vivian as Clarence's best man.

Exterior and interior views of the first O'Mahony lunch wagon built in 1912, as featured in a company catalogue. *Courtesy of Richard J.S. Gutman.*

Vivian Kelly (front row, right), standing outside the Hudson Café lunch wagon, Kearny, circa 1909. *Courtesy of Marilyn Kelly Lamoreau and Joyce Kelly Stanford.*

Joyce Kelly Stanford, the fourth of Vivian's five children, said that her father demonstrated a knack for the diner business and had the discipline, skill and temperament required to manage the demanding workload. She described her dad as a reserved, quiet man, short and bald, with blue/gray eyes. "I always remember him wearing a white apron and a tie. He worked

Kelly's Diner, Kearny, 1923. *Courtesy of Marilyn Kelly Lamoreau and Joyce Kelly Stanford.*

hard and woke up at 5:30 a.m. every morning. He was a whiz with numbers and was a serious, conservative businessman. He did all the cooking."

Vivian was born on September 7, 1884. He listed his "present occupation" as a self-employed "quick lunch" operator on his 1917–18 World War I draft registration card. Joyce Kelly Stanford said that Vivian married her mom, Gladys Wheeler, on January 22, 1913, and of course, Clarence was the best man.

O'Mahony's 1924 catalogue noted that Kelly and Bivens ran their wagon for ten years and then sold it for $1,500, upgrading to a larger O'Mahony diner. In 1923, this new car was installed on the south side of Midland Avenue, on Elm Street—the corner of a residential neighborhood. The diner, now with a fixed location, was dressed down with a large awning and brick walls along its ends and at the front door, apparently to "soften" its commercial image and blend better with the nearby homes.

On February 28, 1949, Vivian opened another new diner at the Elm Street site. A full-page ad in the February 24, 1949 edition of the *Observer* announced the grand opening of "one of the most beautiful and modern diners in this area." This was a glistening stainless steel diner with a large neon sign ("Kelly's") planted on the roof. Outside the dual-door vestibule, neon letters proudly trumpeted that the diner was "air conditioned." Over the course of thirty-six years, Vivian Kelly's business reflected the evolution

Kelly's Diner, Kearny, 1949. *Courtesy of Marilyn Kelly Lamoreau and Joyce Kelly Stanford.*

of the golden age of New Jersey diners—from a small, mobile, wooden lunch wagon to a modern, stainless steel eatery.

During the 1950s, Vivian's children ran the business, especially his second son, Russell, who worked as a short-order cook, and Russell's wife, who served as the cashier. Vivian died on November 28, 1958, at his home in Kearny. Joyce said that he had suffered a stroke several months before he succumbed. Vivian's dear friend, Clarence, attended the funeral. In 1963, Kelly's Diner was relocated to Lyndhurst, at the roadway curve where Schuyler and Page Avenues meet. The stainless steel exterior was covered in brick, and it operated as the Schuyler Diner for forty-seven years, until the summer of 2010, when it was demolished to make way for the construction of the new Schuyler, which opened in July 2010.

On April 29, 1927, the Kearny Power Station unit of the Public Service Production Company of Newark wrote a letter of recommendation on behalf of Clarence. The letter, "To whom it may concern," stated the Kearny Power Station had employed Clarence for the last two and a half years as a chef and restaurant manager, calling him "strictly honest."

Clarence purchased the Butler Lunch Wagon from Joseph McHugh for $3,000 on July 20, 1927, and set up shop at 909 Main Street in downtown Boonton. He renamed the business the Boonton Diner and established a corporation on August 8, 1927, with Vivian as a shareholder. Clarence's business card for the Boonton Diner Inc. read, "We Put the OK in

Right: Clarence Bivens (far right). *Courtesy of Eileen and Peter Glenn.*

Below: Boonton Diner, Boonton, circa 1957. *Courtesy of Eileen and Peter Glenn.*

Cooking" (with the middle "ok" letters in the word "cooking" highlighted). The diner was located next door to Boonton's Harris Lyceum Theater, which was built by George Harris in 1897. The theater housed leading vaudeville acts and movies.

Glenn said that Clarence was active in the community and served as the grand exalted ruler of the Boonton Elks Lodge No. 1405. His business prospered, and in the summer of 1950, he decided that it was time to buy a new eatery—a stainless steel car that was oriented perpendicular to Main

Street. On July 3, 1950, Clarence received a "good luck" Western Union telegram from East Brewster, Massachusetts. It was sent by his friend Albert Peterson, the former mayor of Boonton. The cable read, "May you enjoy much success in opening your new diner."

A fire labeled "suspicious" by Boonton officials destroyed the Lyceum on Saturday, February 2, 1953. A photo in the *Newark Evening News* showed a fire truck parked in the lot of the Boonton Diner, with a ladder extended over the diner that held firemen aloft, battling the blaze. The *Boonton Times* reported that as the fire unfolded, "all occupants of the diner, owned by Clarence Bivens, were ordered out of the eatery and Main Street traffic was closed." Eventually, the burned-out theater was torn down.

Clarence Bivens died on September 20, 1970. He was born on March 5, 1885, and retired in 1960, according to an obituary in the *Paterson Evening News*. In all, he spent more than forty-five years in the diner business. The current diner, located on the Main Street site in Boonton, was installed in the late 1960s/early 1970s, and today operates as a bakery and Latin American restaurant.

Even though they may not have realized it at the time, the pioneering efforts of Kelly and Bivens paved the way for others to follow. They are among the founding fathers in New Jersey's diner history. Their partnership, honorable work ethic and business savvy helped to define a business model to advance that tradition.

Part II

Every Picture Tells a Story

FORTY-FIVE MINUTES YOU'LL NEVER FORGET

In cities, suburbs or on highways, diners provide a level of hospitality that combines the elements of the structure's eye-catching interior and exterior design, tasty food and lively atmosphere. "As a customer, you enjoy the feeling of being in a place where you fit in and can connect with other people," Gutman said. "There's a reassuring familiarity when you become a regular customer. The atmosphere in a diner is informal; much different than being in a restaurant, but there is an expectation of service. You want to be treated in a certain way. It's different for every customer. People enjoy when they can soak it all in—the environment and the experience." Gutman noted that when it comes to diner appreciation, food occasionally is overlooked in the hospitality equation. "People sometimes get carried away with the building design, but without good food, forget it!"

As mobile lunch wagons evolved into stationary diners, they became entrenched in their towns and on roadways as inviting spots to eat, meet and socialize. Don Preziosi, who over three decades has amassed an extensive collection of vintage diner postcards, said that each one is a snapshot of a small, independent family enterprise. In essence, the postcard photos go beyond depicting jazzy structures with neon lights, stainless steel and catchy names. Gutman pointed out that, for diner operators, "this was more than just a business—this was their life." Every picture tells a story—how a person started out at Point A and ended up owning a diner at Point B. These journeys are slices of New Jersey history, told through the story of diners and captured in a single, glossy image.

Diner owners take pride in providing fast service rather than "fast food." In essays posted online, Garbin sought to isolate a diner's underlying essence. It starts with the establishment's intimate interior physical dimensions, which dictate body language and eye contact. Random seating at the counter, where customers are "entertained" by the cooking activity at the grill, precipitates neighborly small talk. (Garbin lamented that many diner restoration efforts eliminate open grills behind the counter.) Then there's the "repose" of booths, where visitors can sit back and maintain a more secluded perch. It's this unrehearsed mingle of patrons that creates the magic inside a diner. A strange human chemistry percolates from this gathering of non-kindred spirits.

"There's always an open invitation to join the theater," Garbin said. "Diners are a haven for humanity. At the best diners, there's never a dull moment. The interaction of people is appealing, and on top of everything, you're enjoying good food. A meal at a diner can be forty-five minutes of your life that you'll never forget."

THE HEARTBEAT OF SUSSEX

Sadie Mae Stronigan, along with her daughters, Madeline, Ruth and Marian, arrived in the village of Augusta in the spring of 1924. She and her husband, Samuel, had owned a dairy farm in Oneonta, New York. Sadie and Samuel were married in 1911, but Samuel died on April 4, 1924. She sold the farm and accepted an invitation to live with her brother, Linden, at his farm in Augusta.

Not long after arriving in New Jersey, Sadie remarried, taking Howard Franklin Weed, a resident of Sussex, as her husband. Because Sadie was a good cook and had experience working in the restaurant business, they decided to open a diner on the town's main thoroughfare, Hamburg Avenue (Route 23). Howard and Sadie signed a conditional bill of sale, dated February 16, 1932, to purchase a Silk City dining car, no. 1087, from the Paterson Vehicle Company for the sum of $9,500, to be paid in monthly installments. Weed's Diner measured thirty-four feet long and just over eleven feet wide, with fifteen stools, an icebox, a steam table, a battery of three coffee urns, two stoves, two sinks and two pie racks.

Howard and Sadie Weed. *Courtesy of Claire Trudgen Dixon.*

Weed's Diner quickly became a popular spot in Sussex. Sadie was the boss and did the cooking, with help from her three daughters. On May 29, 1936, Weed's expanded and celebrated the grand opening of a "dining salon," which could accommodate more than two hundred patrons. The diner remained intact as the front end of the business. A local newspaper of the day, the *Independent*, reported that the Rhythm Boys' Orchestra, led by Buddy Paulison, performed for the festive occasion. "Carpenters and others have been busily engaged in the erection of this new dining salon, which adjoins the present Weed's Diner," the story noted. "The new salon is very pretty inside, with hardwood floors, a soda fountain, and pretty chandeliers." The salon was well received as a place for dinner parties and receptions. The Sussex Fire Department held its annual banquet at the salon on December 30, 1936, which featured a turkey dinner.

Through Sadie's generosity, Weed's Diner quietly fed those less-fortunate souls in the community during the Depression years. Thomas Trudgen Sr., the chief of police of Sussex, carried Sadie's hamburgers in galvanized steel pails to the hobo camp, which was located outside of town near the Tydol Oil facility. Drifters who rode the freight rails that wove throughout the

Weed's Diner, Sussex. *Courtesy of Claire Trudgen Dixon.*

northwestern corner of New Jersey frequented Weed's, showing up to work at the diner for a day in return for a meal. There were several short-line railroads in the area that supported the local dairy and mining industries.

Howard Weed died on March 8, 1940, with Sadie inheriting full ownership of the diner and a 1938 Hudson sedan. Sometime between Howard's death and the fall of 1941, there was a serious fire that damaged the diner and its salon beyond repair. In search of a new diner car, Sadie received a letter from A.E. Cooper of the Paterson Vehicle Company, dated October 13, 1941. Cooper informed Sadie that Eddie's Diner, a stainless steel Silk City car, was vacant and available. "I have a memorandum in our files that if the car ever came in our hands that you were to have first refusal," Cooper wrote. Eddie's diner was transported to Sussex and installed on the old Weed's Diner site.

Sadie continued to operate the business during the war years. In November 1946, she hired George Prout, who was a bombardier for the U.S. Army Air Corps during World War II. Three months later, George's brother, Jack, came to work at Weed's. Following Sadie's death in 1951 at the age of sixty-four, the brothers seized the opportunity to buy the business, renaming it Prout's Diner.

YOU COULD ALMOST see the memories flash before Donald Prout's eyes. He sat in a booth at Atch's Diner in Sussex on a July morning in 2012, just as he did years ago, when this eatery was Prout's Diner, owned and operated by his father, George. The daily grind of running the diner told the story of George Prout's life. A delicious part of that story was when George made his English pasties (from scratch, of course)—the specialty of the house and a Sussex favorite. Pasties are a D-shaped pastry filled with beef, potatoes, onions and butter. "My dad's pasties were never on the menu," Donald Prout said. "They didn't have to be. People in town knew when he was making them. Word got around fast."

The pasties were an important link to George's heritage. He was born on December 3, 1919, in the Cornwall region of England, which is the home of the British or Cornish pastie. The hand-held meat pies were a favorite food among Cornish miners as they were hearty meals that could be brought underground and easily eaten. Thomas John Prout, George's dad, was a miner in Cornwall, and in his day, he ate his fair share of pasties. He brought his family to New Jersey in the early 1920s and worked in the zinc mines of Franklin.

Sussex was a vibrant crossroads in the Skylands region. "People came to the diner for good food and a good time," Donald Prout recalled. "My father had a sense of showmanship. He sang while he was working at the grill." Members of the diverse, loyal clientele were pilots and businessmen who flew in and out of Sussex Airport; Skylands skiers; stock car fans who passed through Sussex to get to the races in nearby Middletown, New York; county and town politicians; police officers; truck drivers; and local merchants. Coffee was $0.15 a cup, and Prout's three-gallon coffee urn was emptied and refilled four times a days. Beef stew dinners were $1.50. The roast beef dinner, with potatoes and vegetables, was $2.25. Burgers were $0.25. British clam chowder was served every Friday. The menu changed every day. Prout's Diner served only breakfast and lunch. "We didn't do supper," Donald Prout said. "Our customers ate their suppers at home."

Donald Prout said that, of all the characters at Prout's Diner, the most memorable was Barbara Davey, a friend of the Weed family. She worked as a waitress, made desserts, was an excellent cook and took lip from no one. A tough, independent woman, customers respectfully called her "Sarge." "She was all business. She was very dedicated; rarely missed a day of work," Donald Prout said, adding that Sarge was more than capable of removing customers for bad behavior. He recalled one instance when, while wielding a meat cleaver, Sarge encouraged an unruly groper to leave the premises in a timely manner.

In 1961, Jack Prout decided to spend more time in Sussex County politics and left the business. Because of the diner's popularity, the amicable split

George (left) and Jack Prout, 1961. *Courtesy of Donald Prout.*

between the Prout brothers was documented in a November 12, 1961 article in the *Newark Evening News*. George also was politically active in Sussex, serving as a borough councilman during the 1960s and as borough mayor (1970–71). He also was a member of the town's fire department and first-aid squad.

During the mid-1960s, Donald Prout, as a teenager, started putting in time at the diner to help his dad—waiting on tables, washing floors, making desserts and peeling potatoes, all done under Sarge's supervision. "We got along great. She would teach me. I listened and learned and said, 'Yes ma'am.'" He compared the family-run diner business to a farmer's life. Donald and his dad woke up at 3:00 a.m. to prepare for the day ahead. Donald was responsible for the deliveries—dropping off hot, fresh food to stores in the downtown business district.

Prout's supported activities in the public schools. Girl Scouts set up tables in front of the diner to sell cookies. Politicians and businessmen negotiated deals over breakfast and lunch. By the end of the afternoon, leftover food was brought across the street to the Sussex Baptist Church to feed those in need.

Donald Prout served eighteen months in Vietnam in the early 1970s and came home a wounded warrior. He and his family sold the business in 1984, two years after his dad retired. George Prout died on January 7, 1997. He was seventy-seven years old. The funeral procession passed the diner on the way to Fairview Cemetery in Sussex. An image of Prout's Diner is etched into George Prout's gravestone. "The diner was the story of his life," Donald said. "It surely was."

The final chapter for the Sussex eatery came when Sarge passed away on June 17, 2000, at the age of eighty-one. More than three decades of her life were dedicated to the diner. Donald Prout became emotional when he recalled the words of his mother (Ruth Zimmerman Prout) at Barbara (Trella) Davey's funeral: "Prout's is now officially closed."

TALES FROM THE HIGHLANDS

The numbers—fifteen stools, 14,600 days, countless conversations and cups of coffee—don't even begin to tell the story of the White Crystal Diner. "My mother's Italian American family fed the people of Atlantic Highlands for more than seventy-five years," In the summer 2008 edition of *Edible Jersey* magazine, Patricia Klindienst wrote an article that recounted the Natale family's history. Klindienst's grandfather, Antonio Natale, who came to New Jersey from Naples, Italy, in 1907, and opened a traditional restaurant in Atlantic Highlands on May 1, 1924, at 81 Bay Avenue at the corner of Avenue B.

The Natale family originally settled in Hoboken and for twenty years ran a restaurant there. A devastating fire in 1929 destroyed the business and the family home. As a result, with no fire insurance, the family was forced to move to a summer home in Atlantic Highlands. Family members worked hard to regroup and rebuild their lives in their new hometown. Not long after they arrived, Klindienst's grandfather and her uncle, Joseph Natale, walked across the Highlands Bridge to the gates of Fort Hancock, an army base. They introduced themselves to the fort's commanding officer and received permission to open a food concession for the soldiers.

Joseph Natale operated Natale's Diner, located on Route 36 in the nearby town of Leonardo, from 1954 to 1959. He and his wife, Carmella (also known as Molly), launched the White Crystal at 20 Center Street, at the corner of Hennessey Boulevard in Atlantic Highlands, in 1960, after Natale's Diner was destroyed in a fire. Built by the Kullman Dining Car Company, the

White Crystal originally was owned by another family and located on South Avenue in Cranford. It operated there for several years but was repossessed by Kullman. Joseph Natale purchased the compact diner, which measured sixteen feet wide by thirty feet in length, and moved it to Atlantic Highlands.

Klindienst said that the story of the White Crystal represents a bygone period in Atlantic Highlands' history, "a small, local business where the owner knew everyone by name. Theirs was a classic New Jersey diner." Twenty-four hours a day, the Natale family welcomed customers and neighbors for breakfast, lunch and supper. The White Crystal's late-night shift ended in 1973 when Joseph Natale died behind the counter of a sudden heart attack while on the job. Joseph's son, Anthony, took over the business with help from Molly.

"Sometimes you don't choose the job; the job chooses you," Anthony Natale said during a January 2013 interview. "I shared a lot with my customers—good times and bad. They were people from all walks of life. You'd have a lawyer sitting next to a sanitation worker, who was sitting next to a businessman, who was sitting next to a high school student. People enjoyed being there. My customers were like family. I knew what they wanted before they walked into the diner. I knew how they liked their coffee. I watched their kids grow up. We served fresh, wholesome food. I learned from my father that besides serving good food, you had to know how to entertain the customers."

By 2000, Anthony Natale knew that his final performance was rapidly approaching and that the show was coming to an end. "It was time to go," he said. "I spent forty years of my life at the diner. It wasn't easy for me to say goodbye. Even today, when I see people around town, they say to me, 'Boy, we miss that place.'"

The White Crystal closed in October 2000. Atlantic Highlands mayor Michael Harmon issued a proclamation honoring the Natale family for "having provided so many meals…and for bringing so much support, life and energy to Atlantic Highlands." An editorial in the October 26, 2000 edition of the *Courier News*, with a byline by former publisher Jim Purcell, marked the passage. A cartoon above the editorial's text depicted tearful residents waving goodbye to the diner, which was flying away from its familiar location via angel's wings. The thrust of Purcell's editorial was that Atlantic Highlands had lost something far more valuable than just another place to eat:

Last week the White Crystal Diner closed its doors during an emotional goodbye to its long-time customers. President Kennedy presided over Camelot and America was still innocent when Anthony Natale and his mother, Molly, served their first cup of coffee at the White Crystal. I do not believe we should allow the passing of the White Crystal to go without mourning a little. American industry did not begin with IBM, Shell, Exxon or Merck; it began with the American small-business owner, waking up in the dark and returning home long after the sun had set. These business owners poured their lives into their businesses and they were part of our communities. They were our neighbors. They lived right next door and we knew them from school. The Natales and their diner are not something we will again see. Well done and best of luck to these fine people.

"I called the publisher and thanked him for that editorial," Natale recalled. "He told me that it 'came from the heart.'"

"Working at the White Crystal made me who I am today," Anthony Musarra said. During his teenage years in the 1980s, Musarra worked at the diner after school and on Saturdays, doing an assortment of cleanup jobs. He described Anthony Natale as being like a protective uncle. "I learned the value of making and saving money," Musarra said. "Having a job taught me how to be independent. I could buy my own clothes. I saved up and bought a nice bicycle. I spent a lot of time hanging around with adults at the diner, so I learned a lot about life from them. As a teenager, I was able to relate with older people."

The adults with whom Musarra interacted usually were part of the late-afternoon crowd of "regulars"—schoolteachers, construction workers and local merchants. "They all stopped in at the diner for a cup of coffee. That's how they wound down their day. It was a place where they could relax, sit and talk. The diner was the social gathering spot in town."

The *Asbury Park Press*, in its November 15, 2001 edition, reported that Anthony Natale had sold the White Crystal property to a local architect, who had plans to build a new two-story structure on the site. The fear was that unless someone was willing to adopt the little diner, it was going to be torn down. Finding a new home and a new owner proved to be difficult. Initially, the White Crystal was moved to a private lot in Atlantic Highlands—a stopgap effort to save it from being demolished—until a local resident contacted diner rebuilder Steve Harwin of Diversified Diners in 2003. Harwin had the diner moved to his yard in Cleveland to begin restoration work.

Meanwhile, Danny Boyle of Springfield, Massachusetts, who was looking to purchase a vintage diner, called Harwin. Boyle traveled extensively for years as an executive in the entertainment industry but decided to make major changes in his life following the death of his father in 2004. "When my dad died, I decided to put my career on hold," Boyle said. "It was time for me to go home." Considering his options, Boyle decided that he wanted to open a small diner in his town as a fulfilling endeavor. He purchased a small tract of land in downtown Springfield (a former car dealership lot), discovered the Diversified Diners website and decided that the White Crystal was the perfect fit to suit his plans for a classic eatery in his hometown. An article in the March 10, 2005 edition of *Atlantic Highlands Herald* noted, "Danny Boyle sensed the little diner's rich history and great business potential."

Harwin said that the diner needed major repairs, especially the rusted, heavy-gauge steel roof. After eighteen months of painstaking restoration, the White Crystal was ready to be shipped to Springfield. Boyle's intention was to run the diner with his brother and a friend, both of whom had experience in the restaurant business. "My diner was going to be the crown jewel of downtown Springfield's north-end restoration," Boyle said. "Diners are sacred pieces of Americana." Unfortunately, an unexpected denial of permits from the State of Massachusetts broke his heart and ultimately prevented the move to Springfield, according to Boyle.

Following this setback, the White Crystal remained parked on the Diversified Diners lot until Vinnie Altier, a restaurateur from Canton, Michigan, contacted Harwin. Altier managed diners and restaurants for thirty-five years and was in the market for a small diner to be situated in downtown Canton. Vinnie's Hamburger Stand was opened on January 1, 2012. The menu is classic diner fare: burgers, fries, chili, soup, grilled cheese sandwiches, coffee and soft drinks. Patrons sit close to the grill and watch their food being cooked, just like diners in the old days, Altier said. "Food is only half the meal. The other half is the diner experience—the character and the personality of the place." Altier said his customers—especially teenagers and young adults—have fallen in love with the eatery and are fascinated by its classic design. "Now these young people know what a real diner looks like," he said. "I admire the New Jersey craftsmen who built this diner. I'm a happy man."

The brave little diner from Atlantic Highlands finally found a home in Michigan. As for Danny Boyle, he opened and later sold a successful restaurant in Springfield: the Common Ground Diner on Main Street. He still owns his piece of property in downtown Springfield and has hopes of operating a diner on the site. Musarra splits his time between New Jersey and New Mexico, working as a national sale representative for a producer of heating, ventilation and air-conditioning equipment. Anthony Natale resides in Atlantic Highlands, enjoying his retirement days.

In the February 5, 1997 edition of the *Asbury Park Press*, Anthony Natale, contemplating retirement, reflected on his experiences at the White Crystal. He said that he was always impressed by his father's skills as a short-order cook. "It was an art form—talking, cooking, making jokes and cracking eggs the whole time." He then spoke eloquently on the diner's place in the community. "The story of any diner is the customers. I've served the working man my whole life and I'm proud of that."

AUNT FRANCES AND UNCLE JOE

It was a family business, and the family extended to commuters, truck drivers, factory workers, nuns and college students throughout Rutherford and East Rutherford. "I loved the diner, and I loved the people," Frances Fazio said. "It was hard work, but we enjoyed it."

Frances grew up in the Avondale section of Nutley, the younger sister of this author's father. She and her husband, Joseph Fazio, began operating the Boiling Springs Diner in East Rutherford in 1948. The boiling springs are natural underground aquifers that gently come up through the asphalt parking lots in this section of southern Bergen County. Each day Frances, a gregarious woman, made her rounds to the small businesses and light-manufacturing factories in the area, taking orders and then returning for lunch hour with baskets filled with food. Weekly requests for homemade pies and cakes were filled for the nuns at St. Mary Parish in Rutherford. Fairleigh Dickinson University students (when the campus was located in Rutherford) used the diner as a spot for an inexpensive, late-night meal. Frances and Joe were especially fond of the students. "We treated them like they were our own kids. We gave them extra bread and took care of them."

"It was a different world back then," she continued, referring to the postwar years. "People today don't understand what it was like. Everyone pulled for each other. We gave people the benefit of the doubt, and they respected us. Our customers loved us. We were part of the community. Joe and I started from scratch. Our customers supported us so we could make the diner bigger. They helped us to buy a dishwasher. We expanded the kitchen and bought a walk-in refrigerator."

Over the years, they curtailed the twenty-four-hour business in favor of breakfast, lunch and early dinner. In the late 1960s, their son, Joe, came aboard and worked as a dishwasher. "I hated washing dishes, so I knew I had to learn to cook and bake," he said. He juggled his high school studies while working as an apprentice baker. His baking repertoire included donuts, Danishes, apple turnovers, cream puffs, cakes and pies, "all from scratch," he said. "We ran an old-fashioned, small-town diner. Saturday was our big day for business. We had fresh fish on Fridays, split-pea soup on Thursdays and every day there was a different special: meatloaf, turkey, ham, roast beef, corned beef."

Besides baking and cooking, Joe learned the human element of the diner business from his parents. "My father knew how to 'read' people. We were successful because of the way we treated our customers. Trust is important. Your customers have to trust you because they depend on having a good meal. I know some people look down on diners. A diner may not be an elegant place, but people who really know diners know it's a place where you can get a good meal and a good cup of coffee at a reasonable price and get a smile."

During the 1970s, Frances used the diner as a home for her Bible study groups. Nieces and nephews were hired for part-time jobs at the diner. At lunchtime, Uncle Joe, a gracious man, approached customers at their booths and offered additional helpings. "Did you get enough to eat?" he asked. "Would you like more vegetables?" Special pies were baked for the Thanksgiving holiday. A regular crew of delivery truck drivers visited the diner during the Christmas season to sing along to their favorite holiday songs on the jukebox.

The diner business eventually became too difficult for Frances and Joe to manage, and they sold the diner in the early 1980s. Uncle Joe died in 1994. Aunt Frances, age eighty nine, lives in Florida. Today, the old Boiling Springs Diner is now a pizzeria, still located adjacent to New Jersey Transit's Rutherford station. Son Joe moved on and started his own business: a popular hot dog truck in Passaic, where he utilized his diner skills.

"When my dad died, I lost my best friend," Joe said. "He taught me my trade. He learned his cooking skills when he was in the army. When I was growing up, he used to say to me, 'Son, you cook better than most, but you'll never be better than me.'" Years later, unexpectedly, one day father turned to son and said, "'Joe, I have to admit it: you do cook better than me.' When my dad said that, it meant more to me than anything."

THE COLOSSUS OF UNION COUNTY

Large diners were the rage during the 1940s. O'Mahony's 1943 catalogue proclaimed the Fairview Diner, delivered to 20 Anderson Avenue in the Bergen County town of Fairview, as the world's largest dining car. The Fairview was eighty feet long, sixteen feet wide and had the capacity to seat one hundred patrons. Fourteen years earlier, the company built the giant Bayway Diner for the Standard Oil plant in Bayonne, which measured fifteen feet wide and sixty feet long.

In 1946, O'Mahony topped the Fairview by building the DeLuxe, an L-shaped diner installed at 1981 Morris Avenue (at the corner of Stuyvesant Avenue) in the town of Union. The diner's dimensions were 80.0 feet in length, facing Morris Avenue, and 53.5 feet to the rear—an overall reach of 133.5 feet. The air-conditioned DeLuxe had a stainless steel interior and exterior, radiant heating built into the terrazzo floor and three banks of skylights. An attached structure that housed the kitchen, bakery, freezers and storage areas was tucked into the "elbow" of the diner.

The midsummer shipment day for the DeLuxe was cause for festivities at the O'Mahony Elizabeth plant—like the launching of a grand ocean liner. Marhoefer recalled that she and her two little sisters dressed up in their best clothes to visit their grandfather's production facility. "We walked right through the office and onto the plant floor," Marhoefer said. "Usually the floor was busy with hammering, saws and other machines whirring and whining, new paint smells and other good manufacturing odors and wood shaving curls and little pieces of tile on the concrete floor. But on that day, the floor was jammed with excited people. The plant's big side door was open, and there, ready to be towed outside into the sunshine, was a huge section of the diner. My grandfather brought us through the crowd to see the monster diner up close."

Union Township building department permits, provided by Deputy Tax Assessor Thomas Beisler, CTA, show that an earlier diner, possibly an O'Mahony Monarch model, had occupied the Morris Avenue site. This eatery also was known as the DeLuxe Diner. Township records show that Frank Priessnitz, a resident of Hillside, received a permit (dated November 11, 1938) to install a "steel-stucco" dining car that measured nearly twenty-nine feet wide by forty feet long. Four years later Union resident James J. Mears bought this "first" DeLuxe and on September 22, 1942, acquired a permit to expand the diner's kitchen. On March 13, 1946, Mears received another permit to install the new, colossal DeLuxe from O'Mahony.

Jim Mears in the doorway of the DeLuxe Diner, Union, 1946. *Courtesy of Don and Newly Preziosi.*

The DeLuxe Diner's grand opening on Monday, August 12, 1946, was a sensation in Union. A four-column display ad in the August 18 edition of the *Union Register* newspaper proclaimed that "the best news in today's paper" was that everyone in town "can sit down at the new DeLuxe Diner, New Jersey's largest and most beautiful diner at Union Center. We are going to try and please you more and more in a quiet and homey atmosphere." A two-column photo in the same edition of the *Union Register* showed Mears posing among local dignitaries, a group that included Union mayor F. Edward Biertuempfel. A related news article reported that Mayor Biertuempfel, at noon, cut a satin ribbon in the diner's vestibule doorway, officially opening the DeLuxe. The story described the massive diner as having a "cream and chrome" exterior, while the interior had a color palette of dark gray with maroon trim, complemented by stainless steel walls and fluorescent lighting. "It furnishes an atmosphere of cheerfulness combined with restfulness," the *Union Register* noted. "Mr. Mears has spared no effort to provide the residents of Union with the finest diner in the state, if not in the entire East." The diner had seating for 152 patrons, with a staff of 60. The DeLuxe did all its baking on site and even made ice cream.

Mears, interviewed for the January 1947 edition of *The Diner* magazine, said that he bought and sold several diners in Newark before purchasing the DeLuxe. Mears was candid about the ups and downs of his early career, saying that he started in the diner business in 1930 as an energetic man in his early twenties but declared bankruptcy after two failed diner ventures. "I was only 23 when that second restaurant failed, and I figured the experience taught me a lot." He found his groove when he opened a third diner in 1932, which was located at the intersection of South Street and Railroad Avenue in Newark, near the city's Ironbound section. He made a key decision to relocate the diner several blocks to a lot on McCarter Highway, a main thoroughfare for the city. The move paid off, and the diner flourished, enabling him to buy another diner, also in Newark. In 1942, he became aware of an opportunity to purchase the "old" DeLuxe Diner in Union. He sold his Newark eateries and acquired the DeLuxe. Now the wind was at his back, and he was on a roll. The *Diner* article noted that, under Mears's leadership, "customers in the [old] DeLuxe Diner stood three deep practically 24 hours a day." The success inspired Mears to "go big" and invest in the new DeLuxe.

The DeLuxe Diner continued its successful run over the next eight years, and the business was last listed in the 1954 Union City Directory. Mears sold the diner in 1955, retired and moved to Florida. A new business, the Union Center Diner, was posted as an entry in the 1956 Union City Directory at 1981 Morris Avenue address. Thomas Beisler said that the new owners kept the existing DeLuxe structure in place, operating the diner under the new name. By 1959, the name had changed to the Kless Diner, and then it became the King's Diner in 1961.

The colossus of Union County was demolished in the winter of 1964. A fast-food restaurant named Goodies was built on the site and operated until June 1974, when it, too, was torn down. Beisler said that the township purchased the property in December 1981. Today, it's part of Union's Columbus Park and also serves as a downtown parking lot.

James Mears died in Fort Lauderdale, Florida, on June 22, 1981, at the age of seventy-three. His obituary in the June 23, 1981 edition of the *Fort Lauderdale News* underlined the biggest accomplishment in his career. "Prior to his retirement, Mr. Mears operated the largest diner in the world in Union, New Jersey."

Goodbye to Rosie

Larry Cultrera is absolutely effervescent when it comes to discussing diners. And as far as possessing an authoritative grasp of the many Jersey-built diners that dot his beloved home state of Massachusetts, you could say that Cultrera wrote the book on the subject. You could say it because he *did* write the book: *Classic Diners of Massachusetts*, published in 2011 by The History Press. He's a member of the Society for Commercial Archeology in Little Rock, Arkansas, a national organization dedicated to the preservation of classic twentieth-century American buildings, artifacts and symbols, and publishes his own exhaustive diner blog (dinerhotline.wordpress.com).

So, what does a guy from the Bay State know about diners in New Jersey? As it turns out, quite a bit. An intrepid traveler, Cultrera has explored the Garden State many times in search of diner experiences. He relishes the prospect of stepping into a diner for the first time and engaging all the sights, smells, sounds, tastes and new acquaintances. "I love the way you can sit at the counter and meet people. I love listening to the stories they tell. That's the Americana element." Breakfast is his preferred diner meal at any hour of the day. "Always breakfast," he said. His favorite order is eggs "over hard" (breaking the yolk), sausage, toast and coffee.

Cultrera was on hand in January 1990 when Rosie's Diner (made famous because of the popular Bounty® paper towel TV commercials) was being removed from its nest on the Route 46 circle in Little Ferry for the hinterlands of Michigan. As a diner aficionado, Cultrera felt compelled to be a part of the grand sendoff. He drove to the Garden State on a Thursday afternoon in a rented van filled with ceramic sculptures he picked up at a gallery in

Larry Cultrera (left), with Tim Kamataris and Gail Kamataris-Prizio at Tim's Diner, Leominster, Massachusetts (Silk City diner car no. 4921), January 12, 2013. *Courtesy of Larry Cultrera.*

Boston for his good friend Jerry Berta, who was about to become the new owner of Rosie's Diner. He met Berta, an artist from Rockford, Michigan, and Berta's pal Fred Tiensivu at Newark Liberty International Airport the next morning in preparation for Rosie's last days in New Jersey.

Berta, Tiensivu and Cultrera parked themselves at a nearby motel and proceeded to help out at the diner by bussing tables and waiting on customers who stopped in for one last meal. Rosie's Diner said goodbye to Little Ferry on January 14, 1990. Cultrera said that departure day was a chaotic scene of curious crowds, flashing police car lights, newspaper reporters, TV cameras and rock-and-roll radio disc jockeys broadcasting live from the scene. Amid the cold and confusion, someone started handing out free rolls of paper towels to all those who turned out for the spectacle.

Rosie's Diner was built in the mid-1940s by the Paramount Dining Car Company of Haledon. The *New York Times*, in a March 15, 1979 feature ("About Little Ferry—Keeping the Diner Griddle Warm with Memories"), profiled Ralph Corrado, the owner of Rosie's Diner. The story described Corrado as a man "with 40 years of diner smarts. He has a balance to his spirit and seems happy with the sunshine coming into his trim diner. Rosie's is a stainless steel gem of a place…one of the old, honest diners, shiny and tubular with frail red neon piping outside. Rosie's is not one of the carpeted new restaurant-freak diners with cocktail lounges. Rosie's is as simple as a hubcap and unpretentious as its own rice pudding."

The *Star-Ledger*, in its January 7, 1990 edition, filed a story just prior to Rosie's departure. The feature stated that Corrado's father purchased the diner in 1945, naming it the Silver Dollar. Corrado took charge of the business in 1960 and renamed it the Farmland Diner, in honor of the many farms that existed in southern Bergen County. Riding the wave of popularity from the Bounty® TV commercials ("the quicker picker-upper"), Corrado christened the diner Rosie's. The *Star-Ledger* quoted Corrado on how he "lovingly maintained the diner" for three decades. However, he and his son, Arnie, had grown tired of the long hours. In 1989, an automobile glass shop, located adjacent to the diner, was looking to expand. Corrado sold the property in October of that year. But Ralph and Arnie were heartbroken, knowing that their beloved diner most likely would be destroyed.

An article in the August 27, 1995 edition of the *Star-Ledger* ("Rosie's Place") told the story of how Jerry Berta, a ceramic artist and restaurateur, discovered Rosie's on his first trip to New Jersey in 1979, searching for diners to photograph. On a return trip to New Jersey in November 1989, Berta learned that Rosie's was for sale. He met with Ralph Corrado and closed the deal in five minutes, buying it for $10,000. "It was like a miracle," Corrado said in the story. "My prayers were answered."

ONCE IN MICHIGAN, Rosie's became part of a tourist park known as Dinerland, which included a miniature golf course. A story posted on the news website MLive (www.mlive.com), dated April 27, 2012, reported that the four-acre property in Algoma Township, near Rockford, which included Rosie's and two other diner cars, had sold for $125,000 in an online auction. The story noted that "the property needs a lot of work." The diner was "closed abruptly" in October 2011 after shutting its doors for a short renovation project. Berta, interviewed in November 2012, said that, except for his emotional ties, he no longer had any connection with Rosie's. He owned the diner for eleven years, selling it in 2001. He said that the diner remains closed and sits on a lot on State Highway 57 in Rockford.

CONFESSIONS OF A SASSY WAITRESS

For Laurie Ross, a waitress with a forty-five-year résumé, it's all about "the rush." It's noontime on a Sunday. The counter is full, the booths are packed and there's a line of people out the door. Two waitresses have called in sick for the day. The diner is buzzing with voices and kinetic energy. Food is moving rapidly from kitchen to customers. For Ross, this is when things get interesting. This is when the performance starts.

"I like the rush," she said. "I was taught to handle the rush with a smile. You get organized. Every move you make has to count. Most of all, don't let them see you sweat. You're an actress. You're on stage. Smile. Everything is fine. Everything is cool."

Laurie Ross at the Monarch Diner, Wayne, on a Sunday morning in May 2013. *Photo by M. Gabriele.*

Ross is well schooled in handling the rush. Her parents, Robert and Claudia, owned Ross Diner, which opened in 1952 and was located at the intersection of westbound Route 46 and Boulevard in the Cherry Hill section of East Paterson. Master Diners of Pequannock built the diner, which originally had a stainless steel exterior, but in later years switched it to a Colonial look. Ross started working as a waitress at age thirteen and quickly learned that she had a fascination for the rush, as well as for the assortment of characters that frequented the place.

"You meet people from every walk of life. In a diner, every customer is treated the same. People who are 'down to earth' appreciate that. Even though our diner was on the highway, it was a local business. Everyone knew everyone. It was a loud, boisterous place." Bartenders and factory workers made up a sizable portion the loyal clientele at Ross Diner, along with a strong following of truck drivers and bus passengers (the diner was adjacent to a bus terminal). "There was one factory in Totowa, and the boss was one of our big customers," she recalled. "Every Saturday morning, my mom would deliver two hundred cups of coffee to the plant."

Bar patrons flooded the weekend graveyard shift at Ross Diner. Area taverns, based on their municipal ordinances, closed variously at two, three or four o'clock in the morning. Ross acknowledged that this wave of customers created a somewhat volatile atmosphere, depending on the levels of blood-alcohol content and the number of go-go girls present on any given night. Ross, on many occasions, had to negotiate disputes. "Yeah, I had to get in between people to break up fights," she confessed, chuckling at the memory. "At least they were respectful towards me."

Her father, Robert Ross, grew up in Miners Mill, Pennsylvania, and left school at an early age to work and help support his family. The Ross clan moved to New York City, and Robert landed jobs in the restaurant business, eventually running his own luncheonette in Manhattan. He redeployed those skills when he married Claudia and moved to New Jersey. "My father knew the business and was very ambitious," said Laurie. "He had an outgoing personality and was active in town politics. He used to speak up at the town council meetings. We had Democrats and Republicans, sitting side by side at the diner, having breakfast every morning."

The early 1970s were a momentous time for Ross and her family's diner. She graduated from Memorial High School in 1972. That same year, the infamous gas shortage hit the Garden State, forcing cars off the road, which cut into the diner's business. As a result, the diner began closing at night. This was a period of economic upheaval for the state. New Jersey began losing its manufacturing base, and many factories in the surrounding towns were shutting down. The year 1972 was also when East Paterson residents voted to change the name of the town to Elmwood Park.

Robert Ross suffered a heart attack in the mid-1970s, forcing him to step away from the business during his recovery. By 1977, Laurie Ross had been thrust into the role of managing the diner. "At that point in my life, I knew how to run the place." She decided to go "old school" and simplified the menu to focus on eggs, burgers and steaks. By the late 1970s, the state reacquired the diner's property on Route 46 to develop a park-and-ride lot. Robert Ross initially considered moving the diner to another location, but then realized it was too cost-prohibitive. In 1980, Ross Diner closed its doors and was torn down. Laurie recalled that there was little drama—no long, drawn-out, tearful goodbyes.

Still attracted to the diner business and the rush, she kept getting waitress jobs: the Suburban and the Forum (both in Paramus), the Arena (in Hackensack) and the Plaza 23 (Pompton Plains). By the 1990s, Ross had decided that it was time to get a full-time, non-diner "day" job, but she still kept her hand in by working as a waitress on weekends.

In the pantheon of Jersey diner waitresses, Ross confirmed that there is an array of classic personality types—from cold, stoic and efficient to frazzled and disorganized; thorny, brusque and intimidating; and sassy and self-assured. "I'm definitely the loudmouth, sassy type," she admitted. "I'm a counter girl. I get to know everyone." She said that, before there was Facebook, Twitter and LinkedIn, diner waitresses were the great networking resource for local social, cultural and business information. Because of their vast word-of-mouth connections, waitresses are often asked to give personal referrals on the best doctors, landscapers, lawyers, car dealerships, wedding bands and real estate agents. It's an interaction she enjoys. However, Ross lamented that some members of the current generation of diner entrepreneurs have little appreciation for this human element—the casual conversations that inspire customer loyalty. "A lot of owners today think it's only about the food," she said. "They miss out on the people side of the business."

Reflecting on her long journey as a Jersey waitress, Ross revealed that there is a melancholy side of the diner business: lonely men. "The world is full of them," she declared. Years ago, she gained a heartfelt awareness for this human condition—a quiet, unnoticed part of the diner scene. According to Ross, these are men who are widowed, divorced or have lost touch with family and friends. Some are in complicated, transitional stages of their lives. Others may travel great distances due to their careers, forcing them to spend extended periods away from their families. Some have little meaningful interaction with people during the day, making the evening hours especially somber.

"They bounce from one diner to another," she said. "If you know a waitress and you're eating at a diner, you're not having supper all alone. At least you have someone to talk to." For these lonely souls, the diner serves as refuge, a comforting way station that offers a good meal and maybe a wink and a kind word from a sassy waitress.

WORKING AS HIS OWN BOSS

On the eve of his twenty-second anniversary (March 27, 2013) as the owner/operator of the White Rose Diner in Linden, Rich Belfer was all smiles. Belfer is a highly focused, multitasking, award-winning, slider-making man who orchestrates his grill with gentle precision.

"My dad was in the restaurant business for fifty years," Belfer said on the first day of the spring of 2013. "My dad retired twelve years ago. He and I ran a luncheonette in Union before we bought this place," he said, meaning the sixteen-stool, stainless steel, flag-flying White Rose. The diner was at its current location on East Elizabeth Avenue when Belfer and his father purchased it.

While he enjoys his customers and the freedom of working solo behind the grill, Belfer admitted that the blessing can "cut both ways. I enjoy being

White Rose Diner, Linden. *Photo by M. Gabriele.*

my own boss and having my own place, but sometimes the headaches and the worries pile up, and you're on your own."

A *New Jersey Monthly* article ("Blue-Collar Burgers") posted online on January 17, 2011, noted that Shelly Belfer, Rich's father, operated luncheonettes in Newark, Clark, Union and Fords. In 1991, Shelly Belfer purchased the White Rose from the Hemmings family, which founded the New Jersey White Rose "System" in 1958. Rich Belfer said that the Hemmings family (brothers Jack and Bob and cousin Jim) owned four White Rose diners: two in Linden (his and one other that closed six years ago), one in Roselle and the oldest one in Highland Park.

GREEK AMERICAN ENTREPRENEURS

The story told by diner owners often involves a journey from a distant shore, such as Greece. It's no secret that Greek Americans make up a sizable percentage of ownership for diners in New Jersey. Theirs is an important chapter in the Garden State's diner narrative. A major wave of Greek immigration to the United States occurred from 1880 to 1915. A second wave came in the late 1950s and early 1960s, due to political turmoil in the Greek homeland.

Tony Spanakos, an assistant professor in the Department of Political Science and Law at Montclair State University, said that the restaurant business, especially diners, provided a "low barrier of entry" for Greek immigrants to gain a foothold in America. "Greek Americans have done very well in New Jersey," Spanakos said. "The Greek immigrants came to America prepared to work." And because of the strong support from family networking and ethnic pride, Greeks soon learned that the diner business offered rewards for those willing to pay their dues.

"The immigrants who came to America were not necessarily business people in Greece. Many lived in small villages. But when they arrived here, they did gain a mentality of owning a business, like a diner. They understood the advantages. They could say it was 'my' business. In the 1950s and 1960s, many Greek immigrants (who had limited funds but strong family support) opened diners in New Jersey. They worked hard and they learned the business."

"The diner business is a Greek success story in New Jersey," declared Dr. George E. Antoniou, a professor in the Department of Computer Science at Montclair. "I truly respect diner people for their hard work, and I admire their achievements in the food industry and their contribution to the American food culture." Antoniou, who is compiling a book on the history of Greek immigration to the United States, said that Greeks acquired their own fruit wagons, oyster stands and small restaurants in lower Manhattan during the early 1890s. This became the proving grounds for Greeks who crossed the Hudson River to explore the Jersey diner scene, according to Antoniou.

"The Greeks in New Jersey came to the diner business through family connections. The Greek islands, like Karpathos, Chios, Andros and Cephalonia, are isolated, little communities. Families develop strong relationships. They intermarry. People rely on each other. Many immigrants who came here didn't have a formal education, but they were street smart and learned how to adapt in America. In many New Jersey Greek families, when the children go on to college and become professionals, they keep their parents' diner business. Why give it up? It can be a gold mine. They can have their profession and still run a diner."

"Greeks like their food," he continued. "In Greece, evening meals are always large gatherings and a big part of family life." Supper typically begins at 9:00 p.m., the preferred time slot for dining, given Greece's warm Mediterranean climate. To satisfy the New Jersey palate, Antoniou said that Greeks learned to prepare traditional American dishes, and then they added their own ethnic touches to the menu, like elaborate salads and stuffed peppers.

Antoniou was able to achieve his goal of becoming an electrical engineer and a college professor by working at the Arlington Diner in North Arlington in the mid-1970s. It was a culture shock, he confessed. "This was the first real job of my life. I was a transfer student and left my family in Greece to come to America. I worked from 8:00 p.m. to 6:00 a.m. as a busboy, and then we cleaned up and mopped the floor. I was dead tired. During the day, I was a college student." When did he sleep? "Hardly ever, very little, but I learned more than most college students. This is how I met people and learned about the American culture." The irony of his story is that Antoniou's father in Greece owned a restaurant, a situation that created some friendly father/son competition. "My father didn't want me to leave Greece, but he understood I was following my dreams."

John E. Sakellaris also followed his American dream and for five decades has climbed the ladder of success in New Jersey. Born on Karpathos in 1943, Sakellaris decided as a teenager to join his friends, who were headed to the United States. He first arrived in America as a Greek merchant marine, "jumped ship" in Perth Amboy and soon connected with family in Hudson

George Antoniou (left) and John Sakellaris at the Lyndhurst Diner. *Photo by M. Gabriele.*

County. In 1961, at the age of eighteen, he got a job washing dishes at Al's Diner on Communipaw Avenue in Jersey City. Today, Sakellaris and his associates own the Lyndhurst Diner and Clifton's legendary Rutt's Hut (home of the "Ripper" hot dogs). In addition, he is the chairman of Pan Gregorian Enterprises, a Greek diner/restaurant cooperative with 750 members. Pan Gregorian Enterprises interacts with vendors—suppliers of kitchen gear, coffee, soft drinks, condiments and dairy products. "We negotiate for the best quality and best prices," Sakellaris said. "We approve the distributors and carry their products, and they get access to do business with members of our organization."

Sakellaris recalled his formative years at Al's, a stainless steel O'Mahony diner. "In those days, when young Greeks like me came to America, the only place to work was in a diner or restaurant. We could communicate in our own language as we learned English." Open 24/7, Al's Diner sold twelve thousand cups of coffee and hundreds of eggs per week and had a loyal customer base of families and factory workers. "We had a small menu," Sakellaris said. "The food was made fresh. Each day, there were specials—beef stew, turkey platters and meatloaf. There were different soups each day, but chicken soup was the standard." The diner had two German bakers who made breads, pastry, pies and cookies. He said that each morning at four o'clock, the entire Jersey City neighborhood along Communipaw Avenue was filled with the intoxicating aroma of delicious things in the diner's oven. "Greeks are good bakers, but the Germans—they're the best."

As he taught himself "Jersey English," Sakellaris began to grasp the tempo of the diner business. During the 1960s, he became a short-order cook. "Most Greek men who work in New Jersey diners learn how to cook in America, not Greece," he pointed out. In 1972, he and three friends bought Al's Diner, and since then, his business career has prospered. In 1973, they purchased Rutt's Hut and then acquired the Lyndhurst Diner. In the 1980s, Sakellaris and his associates sold Al's Diner, which still operates at 873 Communipaw Avenue. The original O'Mahony diner car has since been replaced.

SERVICE ON THE WEST SHORE LINE

The Dumont Crystal, located on West Madison Avenue in Dumont, is one diner that has stood its ground and the test of time. Opened in the late 1920s, the diner originally served commuters on the old New York Central Railroad. Train tracks are located adjacent to the diner, while across the street, running perpendicular to the diner, is West Shore Avenue. The name recalls the New York Central's "West Shore Line" (the western side of the Hudson River), which ran from Albany, New York, to ferryboats in Weehawken. Commuter service began in the 1880s and ended in 1959. Remnants of the old station can be found near the diner.

Dumont Crystal proprietor Momir Saranovic was born in Montenegro, Yugoslavia, on April 20, 1944. As a young man, he trained to be an industrial engineer and arrived in America on December 12, 1967, "the most memorable day in my life," he said with a weary smile. Unable to land a job in his field, he began working at the diner in 1975. "It was the only work I could find," he said, adding that he's only the fourth owner in the Dumont Crystal's history. Saranovic said that the small Bergen County eatery has remained fixed at the same spot for more than eight decades.

The diner's interior is abundantly decorated with framed photos, newspaper articles and other memorabilia. The diner builder is unknown—Saranovic said that a previous owner told him the diner was built in "Hoboken or Bayonne in 1928," which suggests it's an O'Mahony. The barrel-roofed diner has fifteen stools, five booths and a core of loyal neighborhood customers; many have clearance to reach behind the

Dumont Crystal Diner, Dumont. *Photo by M. Gabriele.*

counter and pour their own coffee. Given the anecdotal evidence offered by Saranovic, the Dumont Crystal may be the oldest continuously operating diner in New Jersey.

TICK TOCK

Measured by any yardstick, it's the most acclaimed diner in New Jersey. During its sixty-one-year lifespan, marked by three distinct generations of diner cars, the Tick Tock has hosted truck drivers, high school sweethearts, James Dean wannabes, tie-dyed hippies, football fans, TV personalities, corporate executives, politicians and local residents. It has served up countless hot turkey platters, club sandwiches, Salisbury steaks, regal pies, home fries and oceans of coffee. In the process, it has come to embody all that was, and is, in the mythic Jersey diner saga.

The groundwork for the Tick Tock began on April 30, 1948, when Harry Rutt and his wife, Helen, purchased a parcel of land in Clifton that straddled Route 3 and Allwood Road. Rutt was the younger brother of Royal (Abe) Rutt, the family of Rutt's Hut fame (aforementioned). The 1948 transaction

The original Tick Tock Diner, Clifton. *Courtesy of Jon N. Whiting, Clifton Municipal Assessor's Office.*

presumably was a speculative real estate investment. Considering his experience in the restaurant business, Harry Rutt knew that direct access to a steady flow of automobile traffic was a key to financial success for any future eating establishment.

Swarms of cars certainly were on the horizon. An article in the August 10, 1941 edition of the *New York Times* reported that plans had been finalized to build Route 3, a highway that offered improved access to the Lincoln Tunnel. (The first tube opened on December 22, 1937.) The road included bridges to span the Hackensack River, Berry's Creek and the Passaic River and eventually connected with an extension of Route 6 (today's Route 46) at Valley Road in Clifton. By September 1949, the bridges had been completed, and the final section of the highway, the Nutley/Great Notch section that ran from Cathedral Avenue to Valley Road, had been finished.

Tax and building records from the City of Clifton's municipal assessor's office show that the original Tick Tock, a stainless steel Silk City diner built by the Paterson Vehicle Company, was installed on Harry Rutt's property in 1952. Nick E. Ramoundos and his wife, Katherine, were the proprietors of the diner. Nick's brother, John, also worked there briefly as a partner. Clifton's 1954 city directory, published every two years, lists the Tick Tock as a business at its current site. In 1956, a modular dining room extension was added to the east side of the diner. The Tick Tock was successful, and in

July 1963, Tick Tock Diner Inc. purchased the Clifton property from Harry and Helen Rutt.

Tick Tock owner Nick Ramoundos was a larger-than-life figure, a strapping man with a booming voice, huge hands and a colorful personality. He was everyone's favorite Greek uncle. Born on the Greek island of Andros in 1911, he arrived in the United States in 1932, "jumping ship" from the Greek merchant marines while stationed in Galveston, Texas, a tale he proudly recounted to customers many times over the years. His son Gregory said that Nick hitchhiked to Connecticut from Texas and eventually came to Jersey City, where he worked at various diners and luncheonettes.

Engaging, entertaining and good-natured, Ramoundos also had a private, heroic entry to his résumé. A World War II veteran, he served in the army's Special Forces, making parachute jumps behind enemy lines in North Africa, Yugoslavia and Italy. In 2007, his sons, Gregory and Eric, researched and discovered files on his army exploits, many of which previously had been classified.

The Tick Tock garnered a devoted following. It was the hip place to grab a late-night meal and had an appealing, rough-hewn charm. A sign on the diner's roof proclaimed "Truckers Welcome." The diner had its own ramp and "island" off the shoulder of westbound Route 3 where truck drivers comfortably eased off the highway and slipped into the parking lot.

In addition to the Tick Tock, Clifton was flush with diners in the 1950s, 1960s and 1970s: the Perryman Grill (Lexington Avenue), the Aztec Diner (Route 3), the Queen's Diner (Van Houten Avenue), the Lexington Diner (Lexington Avenue), Scottie's Diner (Main Avenue), the Clifton Plaza Diner (Clifton and Lakeview Avenues), Claremont Diner (Route 3, previously located in Verona), the Melody Hill Diner (Route 46) and the old Allwood Diner (Market Street and Bloomfield Avenue; the new Allwood Diner opened on Allwood Road in March 2011).

By the mid-1970s, change was in the air and on the highway. Five miles to the east of the Tick Tock, at the intersection of Route 3 and the New Jersey Turnpike, the Meadowlands Sports Complex was being built, which featured professional football, harness racing and a multipurpose indoor sports and entertainment arena. Giants Stadium opened on October 10, 1976, drawing more than seventy-six thousand fans. Interviewed by Michael Aaron Rockland for the cover story in the October 1977 edition of *New Jersey Monthly*, Ramoundos said that the opportunity to attract more customers, due to the presence of the sports complex, convinced him that it was time to retire the old Tick Tock and get a larger, more modern diner. Although confident that it was the proper business decision, Ramoundos confessed to Rockland that he had mixed feelings, knowing that the diner's vibe, cultivated over three decades, was going to change dramatically. The Tick Tock's Silk City car was weathered and frayed around the edges—proud, well-worn marks of Jersey authenticity. "The old Tick Tock had been basically blue collar in its appeal," Rockland wrote. "The new Tick Tock is middle class and family centered."

Clifton issued a building permit (no. 13212) on January 13, 1976, to erect a new diner. A full-page ad in the April 6, 1977 edition of the *News-Journal* (a Clifton weekly newspaper) trumpeted the grand opening of the "all-new" Tick Tock Diner, with seating for more than two hundred people. The new Tick Tock, built by Musi Dining Car Company Inc., Carteret, was a boxy structure with large windows and carriage lamps. As anticipated, the Meadowlands Sports Complex was putting more customers in the seats. Business flourished and loyal customers remained true, but there were far fewer truck drivers. The redesigned rooftop sign no longer carried the words "Truckers Welcome." The diner's expanded parking lot, now filled with cars, had little room for eighteen-wheel rigs.

Not long after the Tick Tock removed its red, white and blue grand opening bunting, other eateries were eyeing the same high-volume flow of traffic on Route 3. The initial competition was formidable: McDonald's. The September 1, 1977 edition of the *Herald-News* reported that McDonald's attorneys had issued a request to the Clifton Zoning Board of Adjustment to build a 104-seat restaurant next door to the Tick Tock. As detailed in subsequent news stories, the Tick Tock attorneys counterpunched the McDonald's proposal, describing the dispute as a "fight for economic survival." After three months, the Tick Tock prevailed. The November 17, 1977 edition of the *Herald-News* reported that the Clifton Zoning Board, by a four-to-three vote, denied permission for McDonald's to build a restaurant.

The April 29, 1984 edition of the *Sunday Star-Ledger* printed a large photo of the Tick Tock's departed Silk City car at the top of its "Accent" section, citing diners as a category in the newspaper's series on the "Gems of New Jersey." The article offered profiles of diners throughout the state but had special praise for the Tick Tock, saying that it "has more than just kept up with the population growth and changing trends...it has set the standard for the new American diner." It reported that the Tick Tock "rings up sales of more than $2 million a year." The article also took stock of the diner's year-round, twenty-four-hour business—its rewards and demands. Nick Ramoundos boasted that he didn't need a key for the diner's main entrance, cheerfully implying that the doors and business never closed. Katherine Ramoundos was more succinct, summing up the requirements of diner stewardship: "You don't have a diner; it has you."

Nick Ramoundos died on May 26, 1986. Katherine Ramoundos inherited the diner from her husband. Two years after Nick passed away, Katherine sold the Tick Tock to a family partnership led by Steve Nicoles, Bill Vasilopoulos and Alex Sgourdos.

The third and current chapter of the Tick Tock unfolded on April 11, 1994, as construction workers began disassembling the Musi diner car. A page-one story in the April 12, 1994 edition of the *Record* reported that Kullman Industries Inc. was building a new Tick Tock—a grand 1950s-style diner. The Musi structure was transported to Mays Landing on Route 40, where it became the Mays Landing Diner.

Manufactured in seven sections at its plant in Avenel, Kullman delivered the new Tick Tock to the Route 3 site during the spring of 1994. June 1, 1994, was the grand opening. As promised, the diner—crowned with the familiar Tick Tock neon rooftop sign and "Eat Heavy" clock—glistened with architectural features of neon lights, glass bricks and stainless steel, all of which radiated a classic and contemporary charm. The *Record*, in its June 2, 1994 edition, reported that the new diner had a price tag in excess of $1 million and provided seating for 230 patrons.

The lead feature of the April 23, 1995 New Jersey section of the *Sunday New York Times*, adorned by a five-column photo of the Tick Tock's rooftop sign, reported that "the diner, artifact of American optimism, is alive and thriving in New Jersey." As a tribute to the Garden State's enduring diner spirit, reflected in the new Tick Tock and other diners throughout New Jersey, the *Times* article lauded the sights, sounds and smells of a good diner: "onion-laced hash browns sizzling on the grill; opaque coffee that flows like Niagara Falls and perfumes the air with the zest of caffeine; the clatter of thick china behind the counter; the hiss of Naugahyde upholstery when you ease down into a booth; and the rumble of trucks highballing on the highway just outside."

The *Times* story also noted that to savor a wedge of "mile-high" pie at the Tick Tock "is to partake of a vintage national optimism that knew nothing of cholesterol and craved plenty of calories to grow healthy and strong." Perhaps the *Times*' editors, stirred by the crimson and chrome Tick Tock, saw the article as a moment to step back and reflect on a roadside culture worthy of a serious journalistic review:

There is no state with a more wondrous variety [of diners] *than New Jersey. To this day, New Jersey is a roadside archeologist's wonderland—it's highways, byways and city neighborhoods gleaming with chrome-banded beaneries that hark back to an age of streamlined, high style and three squares a day. As much as diners may seem to be a product of times gone by, new generations of eaters are discovering them, and a new generation of diners is basking in culinary retro-chic. After the excessive fussiness of the recent foodie age, many people crave what diners promise and the best of them provide: big portions, good value and an honest menu. At their best, diners are restaurants we can trust. Regardless of any such* [ethnic or menu] *variations, all of them have one thing in common: there is plenty to eat.*

There's always plenty to eat. Nick Ramoundos's philosophy for business and life, "Eat Heavy," still echoes at the Tick Tock Diner.

Part III

Jersey Makes, the World Takes

Homage to the Old Masters

The Garden State is the "studio" where America's prized diners were sculpted. There were more than twenty manufacturers and renovators that operated throughout New Jersey during the twentieth century. As an industry segment, it was relatively small compared with major business sectors, such as farming, construction, tourism, chemicals and pharmaceuticals. But even though they were small with regard to their share of the state's overall economic output, author and historian Randy Garbin feels that there should be a greater appreciation for the accomplishments of New Jersey's vanished diner builders. They were the creators of the modular, prefabricated masterpieces. "When you talk about what's iconic in American culture, few things rise to the top like an American diner," he said. "Diners are an expression of U.S. style and ingenuity that's admired around the world. New Jersey is the place where most of the vintage diners we know and love were built. New Jersey had the tradition for producing quality, hand-crafted diners."

Some diner manufacturers worked out of makeshift garages and open fields, while others had more elaborate facilities. Diner production in the Garden State has all but completely disappeared, and except for the prefabricated eateries themselves, virtually no vestiges remain of this era. For the most part, it's a forgotten chapter of New Jersey's history. Garbin said that the story of New Jersey's diner manufacturing heritage follows an arc similar to many American enterprises: humble beginnings spurred by a handful of pioneers, rapid growth, market saturation, an influx of external competition and gradual consolidation.

I'm a Manufacturer, Not a Contractor

In the early 1950s, in the Riverside neighborhood of Paterson, Herbert and Gilda went to the Riverview Grill Diner for "Saturday night eggs," the favorite nightcap for their weekend date at the movies. "And we had to be home on time," Gilda said. The diner was located at McLean Boulevard and Fourth Avenue, a stone's throw from the Passaic River. The food was good, and the service was friendly. It was a sign of good things to come. Herbert and Gilda were married in 1956.

Born in Paterson in 1934, Herbert Enyart is a survivor—the last man standing from the once elite group of Garden State diner manufacturers. He has been an eyewitness to the arc described by Garbin. Enyart remains active in the field as the owner and president of PMC Diners Inc., located in Oakland, formerly known as Paramount Diners. He and his son, Edward, do site work to repair and restore vintage diners and serve as consultants on historical preservation projects.

"Yes, I suppose I'm the last in the line," Enyart said during a May 2012 interview in his office. His résumé traces sixty-one years—from the days of booming business and healthy order backlogs to the slow decline of New Jersey diner manufacturing. His career began in 1952 with the Paterson Vehicle Company's Silk City Diner division. Enyart worked on the production line, making $1.40 per hour. "I did everything except weld," he recalled. After ten years, hoping to advance his career in the business, he left the Paterson Vehicle Company and accepted a position with Paramount in nearby Haledon. He was a "saw man," cutting wood and metal for the downstream assembly operations.

Paramount owners Arthur and Darwin Sieber (father and son), who started the business in 1932, realized that Enyart had an innate grasp of mechanical design and blueprints (following high school, he had taken blueprint-drafting classes at a vocational school). Within six months he was running the Paramount shop. By the 1960s, he was running the business. This was a time when the landscape for Garden State diners was changing due to the influx of national fast-food chains. He said that there was a period

Herbert Enyart at his Oakland office. *Photo by M. Gabriele.*

in the late 1960s when Paramount faced serious financial difficulties. "I did what I had to do to keep the company alive."

Enyart cited a patent (no. 2,247,893, "Portable Diner," July 1, 1941), filed by Arthur Sieber, as a major innovation in the diner construction business. He said that as diners grew larger and more complex, it became increasingly difficult to ship them from the factory. Sieber's patent for "split construction," as a way to safely and reliably transport multiple, modular sections, was a boon to manufacturers. Once on site, the sections were connected. In the patent filing, Sieber wrote:

> *In order to house the complete modern equipment under one roof, it is necessary to increase the width of the structure considerably. Such an increase in size frequently prevents transporting the structure over highways and makes it impossible to ship by railroad. The main purpose of my invention is to provide a completely equipped modern diner, which may be transported in two or more sections either by highway or railroad to location…Therefore, by my invention, a modern diner…may be constructed in two, open-side sections.*

The patented design involved "split" diner sections "united along a longitudinal division line into a single structure, a frame for each section comprising vertical supporting members along the two ends and one side, and an open frame free of vertical supporting members along the division-line side," with connecting roof and floor channels.

Looking back on his career, Enyart reflected on the Garden State's legacy of diner manufacturing, which he proudly called a "strictly American achievement." According to Enyart, a "true" diner is a modular, prefabricated, fully equipped structure built in a factory and then shipped and installed on site. "Today, the people who build diners are contractors. I'm not a contractor; I'm a manufacturer. When I build a diner, I'm interested in using every square inch of space." A diner, he explained, is specifically designed to have a flow that encompasses the kitchen layout; counters, stools and booths; and floor paths for foot traffic. The same holds true for the placement of utility lines and electrical wiring.

"Everything has a purpose and place," he continued. "Once it's up and running, when food is being served, when customers are walking in and out the front door, when the cash registers are ringing—that's the flow. All that activity has been engineered to function in a certain way. You learn a lot from your customers, especially when it comes to things like the kitchen layout. In the old days, we designed diners by trial and error. We learned from our mistakes."

HOSPITALITY DESIGN (ON THE FACTORY FLOOR)

Much like Enyart, Frank Conte knows all about flow. When it comes to diner design, Conte considers the big picture but sees it in three dimensions and then thinks about all the moving parts. According to Conte, designing in three dimensions isn't an abstract vision but rather a real-world exercise in "space planning" that balances traffic patterns of employees with the size and placement of kitchen equipment and the layout of a dining area. The goal is to create a space where people can work together and customers can comfortably enjoy a meal.

Born seventy-seven years ago in Minturno, Italy, Conte came to America at the age of two, growing up in East Orange with his extended family. Throughout his life, he has confronted serious illness and physical disabilities, including cancer and a mild hearing impairment. The latter was brought on by a bout of meningitis at an early age. He overcame these impediments to carve out a successful career in the diner manufacturing business.

Conte landed a job as a draftsman at the Fodero Dining Car Company in Bloomfield, two years after graduating from the Newark School of Fine and Industrial Arts. He was introduced to the diner business through a friend named James R. Ducey Jr., whom he described as a "big, strapping, ex-marine Irishman" several years his senior. Ducey had worked at Mountain View Diners in Singac/Little Falls, a manufacturer that closed in 1957. Ducey maintained his

Frank Conte. *Photo by M. Gabriele.*

connections in the diner business and suggested that there were freelancing design opportunities for Conte and him to pursue. The duo began by working out of a second-floor office at the rear of an East Orange furniture store. The rent was fifteen dollars per month, and there was just enough room for a drafting table, a file cabinet and two chairs. "It didn't take me long to learn the workings of diners—space planning for both the public area and the kitchen," Conte wrote in an unpublished memoir. "A whole new adventure had opened up for me."

The handshake partnership between Ducey and Conte did yield sporadic work with two diner producers, Swingle Diners of Middlesex and the Manno Dining Car Company in Fairfield. As he established contacts through this freelance work, Conte learned that there was an opening for a full-time draftsman at Fodero. He applied in the spring of 1960 and got the job. His internship with Ducey opened the door to an unexpected career path, which turned out to be a blessing, according to Conte.

The process of designing a diner began when clients came to the factory to discuss their plans. At Fodero, this conversation included company designers, sales representatives, production foremen and financial staff. This gathering fostered a more comprehensive approach to building a diner, with all players providing input on the front end of the project. For Conte, the conversation started with the diner's proposed menu. "I wanted to know what the clients were planning to have on their menu," he said. "What type of food were they planning to serve? What kind of equipment did they need? I wanted to know where the diner was going to be located, the size of the site and the seating capacity. Once you know all those things, then you can design a kitchen."

After sorting out ideas on food and kitchen equipment, the conversation then turned to the interior space to serve and receive customers—"hospitality design," as described by Conte—and then to the style and materials for the diner's interior and exterior. In essence, during his days at Fodero, he learned that designing a diner was an "inside-out" process, starting in the kitchen and then finishing with how the diner would look from a roadside view. After consulting with clients and revising several working drawings, a final design was submitted to an architect, who reviewed the blueprints and then submitted them to a town to obtain a building permit.

Conte fell in love with designing "moveable restaurants" and with the hospitality business. His approach involved "shop work"—that is, going into the plant's manufacturing area and using crayons to sketch out the diner's layout directly onto the wooden beams of the factory floor. This artistic visualization exercise aided workers, management and diner customers by literally mapping out the diner's dimensions. For Conte, it was all part of the creative process. "I found no boredom with this job. What I enjoyed most was consulting with the customers about what they needed for their diner, trying to incorporate some of their ideas on paper (and on the factory floorboards) so that the job could be priced out."

When it comes to diner design, there's no doubt that Conte comes from the streamlined, stainless steel school. He said that functional hospitality design is an evergreen learning process, as each diner has its own footprint and workflow patterns. Mechanical drawings and measurements on paper must be translated to fit three-dimensional, real-world conditions. It's an art that can be studied and appreciated from many angles. Conte said that the best way for any novice to understand the human dynamics of the diner business is to start from the dishwasher's perspective. "Dishwashers are in the kitchen, and they observe the diner's entire operation. They see and learn how the cooks are working. They watch how the food is being served." Anecdotal evidence suggests that Conte is on target with this insight; a recurring diner success story involves how a current diner owner started in the business as a dishwasher.

By 1967, Conte was feeling "restless" at Fodero and accepted a design position at Swingle. After nearly three years, he moved on to the Musi

Dining Car Company in Carteret. In 1972, seeking more creative freedom and wanting more time to spend with his growing family, Conte established his own business, Designs by Francesco, and worked independently until retiring in 2008. By his count, he has worked on 250 diner/restaurant projects during his career, about one-third of which "never progressed beyond the drawing board." One that did was the Phily Diner in Runnemede, a favorite project for Conte.

JOSEPH P. FODERO, who was a foreman at the Kullman Dining Car Company and worked at Patrick J. Tierney Company, started his own business in 1933. The 1935 Bloomfield City Directory (Polk City Directory) identified him as an "ironworker" in Newark. He built diners on the property of his Bloomfield home at 49 Oakwood Avenue. Fodero entered into a partnership with Milton Glick, who provided much-needed capital. The two renamed the venture the National Dining Car Company and, in 1938, relocated to 55 Delancey Street in Newark. Glick managed the financial end of the business, while Fodero directed manufacturing.

A feature article in *The Diner*'s October 1941 edition said that National had "an auspicious debut" with the construction of a giant diner—measuring 30.5 feet wide and 55.0 feet long—delivered to Old Westbury, Long Island. The article quoted Glick, who praised the expertise of Fodero. He said that National custom-built diners for customers, with no need for "stock" models. "Dining car construction today is advanced beyond what the average dining car man could have or would have believed a few years ago," Glick said. "Yet there is only one thing that builds a good diner—experience. Theoretical engineering is not enough. Present day methods, present day equipment, and experience such as Joe Fodero has gained in his twenty-six years of building better diners, makes it relatively easy for us to solve problems, which other dining car manufacturers are afraid to tackle."

National temporarily suspended its business during World War II, reemerging in the mid-1940s under the Fodero name. A listing for the company at 136 Arlington Avenue appears in the 1955 Bloomfield City Directory, with Joseph Fodero holding the title of president and his sons, Pasquale and Theodore, listed as treasurer and secretary, respectively. Theodore eventually became president of the company.

The Empire Diner, located at 210 Tenth Avenue (corner of West Twenty-second Street) in Manhattan, was among Fodero's most noteworthy creations. Built in 1946, the diner was credited as a focal point in the renaissance of New York City's Chelsea neighborhood during the late 1970s, according to various

Mustache Bill's Diner, Barnegat Light, Long Beach Island. *Photo by M. Gabriele.*

online articles. After appearing in movies and music videos, the diner closed its doors on May 15, 2010. Mustache Bill's Diner, a Fodero car on the northern point of Long Beach Island, survived Hurricane Sandy, which walloped New Jersey on October 29, 2012. The Cardinal Diner, previously known as Paul's Diner, is a small, well-preserved Fodero operating in the Kearny meadowlands near the intersection of Schuyler and Harrison Avenues.

A 1948 stainless steel Fodero car is alive and well on Bainbridge Island, Washington. The Madison Diner, previously known as the Big Star Diner, was opened in May 2011. The car, originally located in Willow Grove, Pennsylvania, operated as the Willow Grove Diner until 1963 and then closed and sat on a vacant lot in New Jersey for more than thirty years, according to a plaque inside the diner. In 1996, a retired airline pilot purchased the diner, disassembled it and shipped it to Bainbridge Island. It was initially opened as the Blue Water Diner but then changed hands several times, closing and opening under various names.

Fodero ceased its operations in 1981. The June 22, 1989 edition of the *Independent Press* reported that Joseph Fodero died on June 14, 1989, at the age of ninety-two. He was born in Calabria, Italy. His son Theodore F. Fodero, a navy veteran during World War II, died on February 14, 2012, at the age of eighty-three.

Renaissance Man

Joseph W. Swingle and his wife, Kay (Bruns), attended a family get-together during the late 1940s. At the time, Joe was working as a math teacher. He had graduated from St. Peter's College (today St. Peter's University) in Jersey City in 1943 with a Bachelor of Science degree in mathematics. Kay was a niece of diner builder Jerry O'Mahony, and this was an O'Mahony family party. Joe and Jerry were friendly in-laws, always enjoyed each other's company, and that night, they engaged in a conversation about business and careers.

Jerry was impressed with Joe's character, education

Joe Swingle. *Courtesy of Elaine Swingle.*

and personality and knew that Joe had served as a communications officer on the USS *Hambleton* (a navy destroyer) during World War II in the Pacific Theater. The small talk between the two men soon evolved into a more serious discussion. Jerry asked Joe how much he made as a math teacher. "Come to work for me on Monday, and I'll double your salary and you'll get a company car," Jerry said to Joe. The offer was too good to refuse, and so began the career of Joe Swingle in the New Jersey diner business. Working as a sales manager at O'Mahony's plant in Elizabeth, Swingle was a quick study—well organized, detail-oriented and with good business instincts and communication skills.

After Jerry O'Mahony sold his business and retired in 1950, Swingle moved on and was hired at Fodero. Elaine Swingle, Joe's daughter, said that after her dad worked as a sales manager at Fodero for three years, Swingle determined that he was ready for a new challenge. He and his older brother, Dallas, purchased land on Route 22 in Springfield, bought a diner from

Fodero and opened Swingle's Diner in 1953. Elaine Swingle said that her Uncle Dallas was in charge of the diner's daily operations, while her father focused more on financial matters and management.

An article in the January 1954 edition of *Diner, Drive-In Restaurant* magazine profiled Swingle's new diner, which was praised as a showcase of design excellence. "After inspecting diners for years all over the country and always trying to improve them, Joe put everything he had into his own venture. The result is an eyeful that merits careful study by other operators." The diner, which measured fifty-three feet in length and seventeen feet in width, was built at a price tag of $100,000. The story said that the diner had a seating capacity of sixty-eight, with twelve booths and twenty stools, as well as a staff of nineteen employees. The stainless steel exterior with inlaid flex glass featured decorative, outdoor, retractable aluminum window awnings, curved corners, a main-entrance vestibule with hoods over two doors and a large sign atop the roof that read, "Swingle's Diner; Air Conditioned." The diner's spacious interior also received rave reviews from the magazine, with a reception area just beyond the main entrance "sumptuously decorated with an upholstered waiting lounge that had thermo-pane glass windows, indirect fluorescent lighting, mirrored walls and tile flooring. Refrigerated display cases for desserts were situated at each end of a long counter. The dining area was appointed with a full-length mirror along the ceiling and two-toned terrazzo flooring."

The third and final stage of Joe Swingle's career as a multitalented diner Renaissance man came in 1957 when he founded Swingle Diner Manufacturing at 300 Lincoln Boulevard in Middlesex. One of his first personnel moves was to hire Elmer Ricter, who had been a shop foreman at Mountain View Diners, which had shut down that same year.

During his years as a sales representative, Joe Swingle studied the factory operations at O'Mahony and Fodero, which gave him a more comprehensive knowledge of the business, Elaine Swingle said. "My father was intimately involved in the manufacturing end of the business. Nothing got by him. He used Jerry O'Mahony's Elizabeth plant as his model. It was a well-planned-out factory. My father wasn't much involved in the design of diners, but he did know about the production of diners."

The first diner produced by Swingle in 1957 was Twadell's Diner, shipped to Paoli, Pennsylvania. Diner car no. 15 was the new Swingle's Diner on Route 22, which replaced the Fodero car on the same spot. Years later, Swingle remodeled Swingle's Diner, giving it a Colonial look. Overall, Swingle produced 147 diners, according to Elaine Swingle. Mike Kelker, who married Joe Swingle's oldest daughter, Margo, became a

Swingle's Diner, Springfield, circa 1953. *Courtesy of Elaine Swingle.*

sales representative for Swingle Diner Manufacturing. The Swingle sales philosophy was based in large part on the business model developed years earlier by Jerry O'Mahony. Selling a diner was just the first step in the transaction. Much like O'Mahony, Swingle provided various support services to the diner owner. The goal was to develop a profitable diner business and cultivate a solid, successful customer base for future diner purchases. "Our business was more than building diners," Kelker explained, noting that he joined the company in 1970. "It was really about picking the right people to run a diner in the right place. It was all about helping to put people into the diner business and making them successful. We stood behind them. It took time to build a sense of confidence with people in the market. Your word was your bond."

There were specific financial metrics that reinforced this goodwill business policy. Kelker and his sales associates collaborated with the diner owners to analyze food costs, salaries, rent, equipment depreciation, state and local taxes and utilities to determine a break-even point. This cooperative effort yielded the detailed financial information that Swingle and diner owners presented to a bank to help the diner owner obtain a loan to start the business.

"Diners really began to change a lot after World War II, when the short-order cook in front of the diner moved into a kitchen behind the doors," Joe Swingle was quoted as saying in an October 23, 1983 feature in the *New York Times Magazine.* "In many ways, they started to resemble restaurants." The article discussed how the diner scene was in a period of transition and how the menu, appearance and clientele had drifted away from the streamlined, stainless steel era. However, the feature also identified an emerging trend: a nostalgic yearning for the more retro look of the 1940s and 1950s.

At the age of twenty-one, Joe W. Swingle Jr. took over Swingle's Colonial Diner on February 5, 1975, establishing a partnership with cousins Dallas Jr. and Shawn, as well as other family members. Prior to this move, Joe Jr. had worked several summers at the diner manufacturing plant. In early 1975, the Swingle diner was put up for sale, and Joe Jr. decided that it was his opportunity to jump into the business. He worked for one year, with no days off, twelve to fifteen hours a day, and was able to repay his father for the collateral used to restart the business. "That was a proud day in my life," he said.

When Joe Jr. first took over the managerial duties, the diner's business was "hovering around the break-even mark." He said that he initially focused on reducing labor costs and improving service and food quality. Dallas left after working for a year, but Joe Jr. and Shawn carried on. "Business was profitable and supported our families," he said. "The last two years, we lost our focus and the business suffered."

During his years at the helm, Joe Jr. said that his dad was "cautious with advice. He didn't offer too much other than, 'Don't be bashful about raising menu prices.'" After managing the diner for twelve years, Joe Jr. closed the business. The Swingle Colonial diner was removed, the property was sold and the site became a car dealership.

In the early 1980s, Trenton passed legislation with unintended consequences for the diner business, adding complexity to the building codes, regulations and taxes that affected the "modular construction" industry, according to Kelker. These regulations drove up costs to build and buy diners. He said that the new codes also greatly inflated the time required to obtain building permits and get site-selection plans approved.

Swingle Diner Manufacturing built its final three diners in 1988: the Stagecoach, shipped to Brunswick, New York; the Plaza View, sent to Closter; and the American Diner, sent to Philadelphia. Later that year, Joe Swingle closed the manufacturing plant and retired from the business. He died on June 16, 1989, at the age of sixty-eight. His daughter, son and Kelker all lauded Swingle for his business savvy, integrity, family values and the versatility he demonstrated in every phase of the diner business.

"Joe Swingle had a magnetic personality," Kelker said. "He had a great sense of humor, a sharp memory and he knew his business. People enjoyed working with him. When you did business with Joe, you had a sense that you could trust him."

Mandolin Music

Erwin C. Fedkenheuer was enjoying a cup of coffee and a toasted corn muffin at the Bendix Diner on Route 17 in Hasbrouck Heights one Tuesday morning in early October 2012. For more than thirty years, this was the daily ritual for Erwin and his dad, Erwin W. Fedkenheuer, to start their day at Erfed Corporation. Based in Rutherford, Erfed rebuilt and remodeled diners. Erwin's dad started the company in 1956 with an investment of $10,000. The business was located on Route 17, not far from the Bendix, at the site of the old Bonnie Dell Dairy Farm. The staff included four sheet metal workers and one carpenter.

Erwin Fedkenheuer at the Bendix Diner. *Photo by M. Gabriele.*

The company identified diner remodeling as its business niche. Erfed's initial assignments included refurbishing Rusell's Diner in Cliffside Park and Hollis Diner in Queens, New York. "We were a small company," Erwin said. "Remodeling was the work that came our way. We retrofitted windows, rebuilt vestibules and repaired roofs. That's how our company developed."

Erwin, the son, was born in Jersey City on December 30, 1931; grew up in Hoboken and Passaic; moved to Carlstadt in February 1945; and graduated from Fairleigh Dickinson University, Rutherford, in 1952 with an industrial engineering degree. He served in the army for two years, took advantage of the GI Bill, went back to Fairleigh Dickinson and earned a business administration degree. He then took a job as a spot welder at the Midway Company on Garabaldi Avenue in Lodi; the company assembled aircraft parts as a vendor for the Curtiss-Wright airplane engine factory in Wood-Ridge. He utilized this metalworking experience when he and his dad decided to launch Erfed Corporation.

Growing up in Germany, the elder Fedkenheuer was an apprentice to a sheet metal master craftsman and then became a plumber, which was a natural career progression during those years. In addition to his superior metalworking skills, Erwin's father also loved playing the mandolin, which turned out to be a key factor in his decision to come to America:

> *My father decided to follow his buddies from Germany, and they all came to Hoboken to work in America. These were his best friends, and they all enjoyed playing music. That was how they had fun in those days, and that was a big reason why my father decided to come to the United States—to be with them. The story he told me is that right after they arrived in Hoboken, they all got together and took a trolley to a bar in Carlstadt* [a German-immigrant enclave in southern Bergen County]. *They played mandolins and caroused all night. They were happy to be together in America.*

During the early 1930s, the elder Fedkenheuer was employed at Blichmann, a metalworking company in Weehawken. His specialty was working with stainless steel, and he built large metal coffee urns. In the 1940s, Arthur Sieber of Paramount Diners was introduced to Fedkenheuer. Sieber was impressed with the elder Fedkenheuer's work as a stainless steel artisan. Most likely, Sieber purchased several stainless steel urns from Blichmann to install in Paramount diners. Erwin's father went to work at Paramount, making seventy dollars per week, and quickly rose to the rank of shop foreman.

As Erfed's business grew in the late 1950s and early 1960s, the company built several diners, including Shirley's in West New York, the Bel Air in East Rutherford and the 14th Street Diner in Hoboken. Erwin gradually took on more managerial responsibilities, and by the mid-1960s, he knew that the diner business was fading. "You could see it coming," he said. "We were the established company, but people were underbidding us for remodeling work. The prices they were quoting—it was impossible for our competitors to make money." Their presumed reasoning, he said, was that the competition wanted to break into the market, hoping for an upturn in the business that never came.

Erwin's dad died on January 18, 1989. As diner contracts diminished, Erwin steered the company into the construction of modular metal concession stands and stainless steel food vendor wagons for sports stadiums. One of Erfed's last jobs was an order for concession stands at Camden Yards baseball stadium in Baltimore. He closed the shop in 1999 and retired.

"My dad and I remodeled dozens of diners over the years," he said at the Bendix in between bites of his toasted corn muffin. "We worked on all types of diners with different designs. It was a good business while it lasted. I'm proud of what we accomplished."

Erwin took his last sip of coffee and smiled. For a brief moment, in between the *whoosh* of cars on Route 17, you could almost hear the faint, sweet sound of mandolin music in the distance.

THREE GENERATIONS

A reporter for *The Diner* paid a visit to the Kullman Dining Car Company in Harrison and filed a story in the trade magazine's February 1941 edition. The article painted a flattering portrait of company owner and founder Samuel Kullman. "Dressed in good taste, only the gray of his hair belied the extremely youthful appearance of the man who founded the company and has been its president since it was formed 14 years ago."

Kullman was quoted as being upbeat about the diner industry and anticipated vast opportunities for business outside New Jersey. "I recently

Kullman promotional flyer. *Courtesy of Don and Newly Preziosi.*

made a trip around the country and found that, west of the Mississippi, a modern deluxe diner was a rarity. With the advance of industrialism throughout the South and Midwest and the heavy traffic on our well-traveled highways, the dining car industry will come into its own, and the future appears bright for both the manufacturer and the operator."

He provided a tour of the Harrison plant for the reporter, pointing out various state-of-the-art manufacturing stations on the factory floor:

> *The skeleton and under-structure* [of our diners] *is entirely of steel. The exterior is covered with porcelain and stainless steel trim or entirely of stainless steel in various designs. The windows have the latest-type aluminum frames and the doors are stainless steel. The interior is tiled in various designs and the ceiling is either of porcelain or various marble effects or Formica. All our equipment is of stainless steel, heavy gauge, including stainless steel hoods and menu signs. For ornamental effects, we use glass blocks and fluorescent lighting. Kullman deluxe diners include air-conditioning systems that change the air in the diner every 30 seconds and keep it free of cooking odors.*

At the end of the article, Kullman tipped his hand on a new product line being developed by his company: a small, medium-priced diner car. He said that this new model utilized the same construction materials as the larger Kullman models but wasn't a "sectional" diner; rather, it could be shipped by truck or rail as a single unit. The one-piece diner "was ready for business the day after it arrived at its destination," Kullman explained. Gutman wrote that, following World War II, "a new crop of small diners sprouted for returning vets to invest in." He said that one example was the Kullman Junior.

Samuel Kullman and his family emigrated from the Ukraine in the early 1900s. His father was a tailor. Samuel earned an accounting degree from New York University and joined diner builder the Patrick J. Tierney Company in New Rochelle, New York. He quickly was running the business for Tierney, becoming the vice-president of finance, while Angelo DeRaffele—who went on to establish his own diner building company, also in New Rochelle—was a shop foreman.

In 1927, Samuel Kullman founded the Kullman Dining Car Company. The business originally was based in Newark on Frelinghuysen Avenue and then moved across the Passaic River to Harrison. In subsequent years, in need of larger production facilities, the Kullman manufacturing operations relocated several times, to Avenel and eventually to Lebanon. Samuel's son, Harold, joined the business in 1946 after graduating from Bucknell

University, Lewisburg, Pennsylvania. Harold Kullman served in the Ninth Army in Europe during World War II. Samuel Kullman retired in 1968 and died on April 6, 1973, at the age of seventy-four.

Over a period of seventy-nine years that spanned three family generations, Kullman was a prolific builder of diners and acquired the reputation for high quality and attention to detail over a broad spectrum of sizes and styles. "Selling diners was a word-of-mouth business," Harold Kullman said during a 2013 interview, recalling his years on the road during the 1940s and 1950s, driving through New Jersey, New York, Pennsylvania, Maryland and Massachusetts to follow sales leads. "Most of the diner builders were based in New Jersey, so selling diners was a very competitive market." Many times, the sales pitch involved negotiating with owners of small, older diners, explaining the advantages of moving up to a larger, modern diner car, which meant more customers and larger profits. Kullman took the old diner as a trade-in allowance and then designed and built a new diner. The old diner was refurbished and then recycled to someone just starting out in the business.

Harold Kullman said that a diner was considered personal property, like owning a boat or a car. Buying a diner involved a "chattel mortgage" or security agreement. "This was a very affordable way for someone to go into the diner business. The diner owner leased a piece of property. We sold the diner on a security agreement, which was used as collateral for a bank loan. If the diner failed, we [Kullman] bought back the security agreement." In addition, vendors (jukeboxes, soft drinks, cigarettes, food, coffee and condiment suppliers) provided financial support so that diners carried the vendor's product lines. "Owning a diner was a great business. If you didn't have much money but were willing to work hard, you could become a millionaire."

During the 1960s and 1970s, diners kept getting larger and more expensive to build. It became difficult to find takers on the trade-ins of the old diners. Banks required more detailed financial information from the proprietors. "Diner owners started buying the land, rather than leasing it, and did more conventional financing," Kullman said. Because the trend shifted toward larger diners dedicated as permanent structures, the preference was to build the eateries on site rather than inside a manufacturing plant.

An article in the October 29, 1990 edition of the *New York Times* cited Harold Kullman and his wife, Betty, for pioneering the shift to Colonial- and Mediterranean-style diner designs—replacing stainless steel exteriors in favor of brick, stucco and stone façades. Diner interiors were also transformed to accommodate family-friendly, restaurant-style seating. This change in design concept for diners, in part, was being driven by outside forces. Gutman wrote:

> *Diners wanted to get away from the fast-food image, so the trend was toward more conservative designs and, on the interior, more dining room and less diner. With the widespread urban renewal projects that ushered in the 1960s came scores of city planning boards, which began to legislate taste in buildings. This was an ominous sign for diners, as the old flashy look was often no longer tolerated. In some regions, all-new diners had to conform to stringent regulations, which often banned not only stainless steel buildings, but even the word "diner." The public response to the Colonial diner was very positive, and many old-style diner owners wanted to redo their places or replace them with new Colonial designs. As the public was enticed with more fast-food choices, the diner was striving to be more than a roadside restaurant. The image was that of a conservative, family-oriented place to eat.*

Gutman credited Kullman with building the first Colonial-style diner with an all-brick exterior. The year was 1962, and the diner was installed in Ocean City. He quoted Harold Kullman, who explained that Ocean City officials frowned on "the jazzy look, so we designed a brick diner that wasn't a diner, but a restaurant." This was a period when municipal planning boards no longer wanted stainless steel diners in their communities. Many townships felt that the 1950-style diners carried a negative, "truck stop" image and no longer fit with master plans for future township development.

Robert Kullman, Harold's son, joined the company in 1969, and as his managerial responsibilities grew, he led Kullman's shift to explore business in non-diner markets. His strategy involved taking the prefabricated, modular manufacturing concept for building diners and applying it to other markets— schools, dormitories, prisons and even offshore embassies, working through the U.S. State Department. It was clear to Robert Kullman that, looking ahead, diners would be just one of many markets for the company.

He became president and chief executive officer in 1989. By the early 1990s, his vision for the company's diversification into new fields of construction had begun to pay dividends and draw media attention. The aforementioned October 29, 1990 article in the *Times*, which carried the headline "Diner Maker Ends Era," reported that because orders for diners had plummeted, the company was redeploying its modular manufacturing expertise to construct prefabricated prisons. "The shift from roadhouse to the 'big house' came under the direction of [Robert Kullman]." The story noted that the company, which had produced thirty to forty diners per year during the 1940s and 1950s, saw diner orders dwindle to just two by 1988.

The June 6, 1993 edition of the *Star-Ledger* reported that Kullman had "carved out a modular niche from roadside diners to embassies." The story noted that the company's business—a diversified portfolio of construction projects—had achieved annual revenues of more than $20 million. "Kullman has built its revenues, added jobs and gained national recognition for pushing modular construction into new markets."

The *Times* revisited Robert Kullman and published a feature in its July 18, 1993 edition, "Diner Builder Takes a New Tack," which reviewed the company's unfolding strategy. "Right up until 1969, we just built diners," he said in the article. "After that, 80 percent of our business was diners, and after about 10 years it flipped. About 20 percent of our business now is diners." The article observed that it was the "20 percent" that made the Kullman name dear to the hearts of diner lovers. Kullman went on to say that the construction of modular telecommunication shelters had become an especially lucrative field. "We just finished 50 [shelters] and we've got an order for 30 more."

He also won accolades from *Inc. Magazine*, which named him the 1992 "Entrepreneur of the Year" for the construction industry. *New Jersey Monthly* magazine, in its January 1991 edition, lauded Kullman as its "business leader of the year" in the Garden State's manufacturing sector.

While appreciating the media coverage, Kullman said that his only regret is the incorrect perception that the company had abandoned the diner business. "We never stopped building diners," he declared during an interview in January 2013. "The diner business did change. Diners became one of our markets, not our only business. We built our last diner in 2005 [the Silver Moon, which was shipped to Baltimore]. We also did diner remodeling work. If I were in business today, I still would be building diners, even if it was only one or two a year, because that was the company's heritage."

Kullman relocated to Lebanon from Avenel in 1995. In the 1990s and early 2000s, the company created stunning diners, such as the third-generation Tick Tock in Clifton. Six miles west of the Tick Tock, Kullman rebuilt and redesigned the Golden Star Diner, located on Route 46 in Little Falls, transforming it into the Park West Diner. The Park West held its grand opening on August 12, 1996, complete with a proclamation by then Paterson mayor William Pascrell Jr. On October 23, 2001, Montclair State University opened the 2,775-square-foot Red Hawk Diner, which was delivered to the campus via six flatbed trucks from Kullman's Lebanon plant.

The company also embarked on an international concept for retro-style diners through an alliance with American Restaurant Concept (ARC), Stuttgart, Germany. The October 7, 1999 edition of the *Hunterdon County Democrat* reported that the Germany enterprise ordered three "Sam Kullman Diners," the first of which was installed in a suburb of Berlin. The article quoted an ARC executive, who explained that "Europeans crave the American lifestyle and the diner provides a natural introduction to the American culture."

Robert Kullman sold the family business in February 2006, and the new owners stopped building diners. NJ.com, in an online article posted on December 9, 2011, reported that Kullman Building Corporation ceased operations and was selling off its production equipment. Kullman expressed pride in the company's legacy and was philosophical on New Jersey's place in history as the center for diner manufacturing. "The era of factory-built diners—that's over. But people are still building new diners on site. There are many diners that need to be remodeled. The story of diners in New Jersey hasn't come to an end."

YARD WORK IN PEQUANNOCK

As he stood on the deck of a steamship bound for New York City, sixteen-year-old Arthur Schelling looked westward and reminisced about his parents and four sisters in Berlin, Germany. Perhaps he had a few second thoughts about his decision to leave his family and seek his fortune in the United States. The year was 1901, and not long after disembarking from the ship, he talked his way into getting a job as a bartender at a German restaurant in Manhattan. It was good start for a young man who would go on to establish Master Diners.

Industrious and charming, Schelling prospered in New York, and by 1913, he had an apartment at 1825 Amsterdam Avenue, along with his own luncheonette on the same boulevard. Seven years later, Schelling, wife Margaret, daughter Elsie and son George moved to a cold-water flat at 535 Palisade Avenue in Jersey City, where he owned and operated a bar. The stay in Jersey City was brief; in 1921, Schelling relocated his family to the country village of Pequannock, located along the Newark-Pompton Turnpike.

Schelling ran a deli in Pequannock on Irving Street and adjacent to the family home. Eighty-nine-year-old Bill Schelling, interviewed in May 2013, said that his father was a good cook, had a mischievous sense of humor and was hired as a salesman for Paramount Diners in the early 1930s. After working at Paramount for a few years, Arthur Schelling left the company to start his own business, building his first diner in 1937 for Mr. McCracken, which became the Newton Diner. The structure still exists today as Brenda's Diner in downtown Newton on Spring Street. The diner was built in Pequannock in a yard on Schelling's Irving Street homestead. It was an outdoor production venue, and this initial project set the stage for more diners to come. A Paramount foreman named Les Daniel, who went on to form Mountain View Diners, built McCracken's diner with Schelling and a small construction crew.

Bill Schelling said that his father completed "about four" diners, with each one taking five months to build. Arthur bought additional property along Irving Street and in 1940 decided to incorporate the business, naming it Master Diners. The Circle Diner, located at the Route 46/Route 23 circle in Wayne, and Teachin's Diner, located on Route 4 in Bergen County, were among the early eateries constructed by Master. Master Diners followed a standard design, based on drawings by Schelling's son-in-law, Goethals Van Lenten. Bill Schelling said that the diners were sixteen feet wide and up to fifty feet in length, with an optional center vestibule.

Arthur's older son, George—who served as an army combat engineer with General George S. Patton's Third Army, building troop bridges in Central

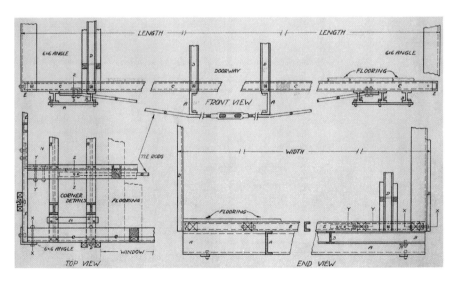

Mechanical drawing showing the structural steel framework for Master Diners, by Goethals Van Lenten. *Courtesy of Jim Van Lenten.*

Master Diners, Pequannock yard. *Courtesy of Carol Magazino.*

Europe during World War II—returned to Pequannock in 1945 and joined his father's business. Younger son Bill was the sheet metal man, bending, cutting and pressing stainless steel. The diners were built al fresco, although Master did have an office, a warehouse and a workshop. In addition to Arthur's two sons, the Master Diner work crew, which included area residents Harry Wright and twin brothers Bob and Ralph Cottrell, typically consisted of several carpenters and other part-time helpers.

In 1947, Master constructed the masterpiece in its "Enduro" line—the Bendix Diner, located in Hasbrouck Heights at the intersection of Routes 17 and 46. Carl DeLorenzo was the owner of the Bendix, which was named after nearby Bendix Airport. The airport, originally called Teterboro, briefly changed its name to Bendix in 1937 in honor of the Bendix Aviation Corporation, which located its Eclipse-Pioneer Division adjacent to the airfield, according to Henry M. Holden and his 2009 book *Images of Aviation: Teterboro Airport.* In 1943, town residents voted to restore the Teterboro name. Like the Bendix, another Master Diner still going strong is the Egg Platter on Crooks Avenue, located along the Paterson/Clifton border. This diner originally was known, appropriately, as Geier's City Line Diner.

The largest diner produced by Master was the Wm. (William) Penn Grill, which was delivered by truck in two sections, each forty feet in length, to a site at 1074 Frankfort Avenue in Philadelphia. In 2000, one Master creation, Al's Diner in Chicopee, Massachusetts, was added to the National Register of Historic Places. According to information on the registration form, Al's,

Geier's City Line Diner (today known as the Egg Platter), Crooks Avenue, Paterson. *Courtesy of Jim Van Lenten.*

originally known as the White Diner, was brought to Chicopee (14 Yelle Street) in 1958.

The Master crew worked outdoors year round in the Pequannock yard. "The diner business was feast or famine," Bill Schelling said. "Either we had too much work or not enough." When asked whether, at the time, they were aware that they were building eateries that would one day become revered structures, Bill shook his head and answered modestly, "No." "We were in business, and we were building diners that our customers wanted. We didn't think it was anything special." He did admit that his dad, Arthur—famous for wearing his trademark bow ties—was a special guy. "He was a character. My father was a good talker and a good salesman. He knew how to make people smile."

Arthur Schelling suffered a heart attack in 1955, which forced him to curtail his role with Master Diners. Sons George and Bill decided to rename the company New Master Diners, and the first booking under the new handle was for a diner shipped to Syosset, Long Island, New York. The last complete diner built by New Master was the Top Hat Diner, which was located on Route 46 in Wayne near the state motor vehicle inspection station. When the Route 46/Route 23 interchange was reconfigured, the diner was moved to northbound Route 23 in Wayne, near Packanack Lake Road. Once at its new site, the Top Hat was renamed the Spindletop Diner and later became known as the North Star 23 Diner. Today, the location is occupied by a colorful retro eatery named Burger DeLuxe, which was opened in September 2008.

The diner market became sluggish in the late 1950s, and Master focused on renovating existing diners, which were brought to the Pequannock yard. During this period, Master also produced several Carvel Ice Cream stores, which echoed the diner look with extensive use of stainless steel, porcelain enamel trim and ceramic tiles. In addition, Bill and George were contracted to refurbish several Silk City diners on site.

By the early 1960s, New Master Diners was dissolved as a corporation, as the Schelling brothers dropped the "New" in the business title, reverting to the name Master Diners. Arthur Schelling died in Florida in 1961. Not long after that, Bill and George decided to end their diner work when they were contracted to remodel cafeterias and guardhouses for the United Parcel Service of America Inc. (UPS) headquarters in Manhattan. The brothers retired in 1969. George, six months away from his 100th birthday, died on January 20, 2013.

Bill Schelling spends the winter months in Florida and returns to New Jersey for the balance of the year to enjoy the company of friends and family members who were involved in the Master Diner enterprise. The diner business remains close to his heart. A remnant of his diner days is on display at his home in Wayne: his kitchen walls are decorated with a polished stainless steel "checkerboard quilt."

SILK CITY

Alexander Hamilton, the colonial-era visionary who helped establish Paterson as a manufacturing center, would have been proud to grab a cup of coffee in any Silk City diner. Founded in 1792 and famous for its majestic seventy-seven-foot-high waterfalls, as well as industrial achievements such the Colt revolver and the Holland submarine, Paterson was home to diner production by the Paterson Vehicle Company for four decades.

Located in a three-block complex at East Twenty-seventh Street and Nineteenth Avenue in downtown Paterson, the origins of the company date back to 1886, when it was founded by Everett Abbott Cooper as a wagon-building factory in Suffern, New York. Cooper, in the late 1890s, relocated the business to Paterson, establishing it as the Paterson Wagon Company. A handwritten correspondence, dated November 28, 1896, on company letterhead, reveals that the first Paterson plant originally was located at 257/259 Market Street. The letterhead logo listed the company's product lines: carriages, business wagons, harnesses, horse goods and bicycles. As mentioned earlier in this book, given these capabilities, the company may have built customized lunch wagons that predated those from Jerry O'Mahony's early Bayonne operations.

Everett Abbott Cooper. *Courtesy of Les Cooper.*

An article in the September 30, 1905 edition of the *New York Times* reported that Paterson Wagon had filed for bankruptcy protection in U.S. District Court in Elizabeth. The following year, it reorganized and reemerged as the Paterson Vehicle Company. It retooled its factory to produce bus, car and truck bodies. Five of Everett Abbot's sons (Abbott Everett, William, Fred Everett, Irving Brooks and Everett Reynolds) held executive positions with the company.

Company treasurer William Cooper led the effort to explore diner manufacturing. Les Cooper, family archivist and great-grandson of Everett Abbott, said that William, after serving as a soldier in World War I, came home to the business and set aside a section of the Paterson plant for a diner pilot project. Interviewed in 2013, Les Cooper pointed to two marketing documents that describe the company's foray into diners. The first noted that Paterson Vehicle had tracked "the development of the dining car and saw in it a product that could be improved by our auto-body building experience. So in the year of 1924 the first dining cars were put into production in our

The White Horse Diner, an early Silk City car. *Courtesy of Don and Newly Preziosi.*

large and modernly equipped factory." He said that this statement referred to the initial rollout of the company's diner prototypes. A second document indicated that full commercial manufacturing of Silk City Diners began in 1926 as a dedicated division within the Paterson Vehicle Company. The business unit was named in honor of Paterson's silk mills.

"Building diners was only a small leap in technology for Paterson Vehicle," Les Cooper explained. "The company was always adapting to the newest mobile transportation platform technologies of the times. They went from wagon and coach manufacturing in the latter nineteenth century to car and truck bodies in the early twentieth century. They even become the distributor of the Ward Electric Car [1915–16], which had an Edison battery. From there they expanded into diner production."

Irving Brooks Cooper (Les Cooper's grandfather) filed a U.S. patent (no. 2,145,919) on April 27, 1938, for diner "vehicle body construction." It was published in the February 7, 1939 edition of the *Official Gazette of the United States Patent Office*. In the patent filing, Irving wrote that his design involved "improvements in the elongated frame structure of a [diner] car body… [that] strengthen the structure without the presence of underneath trussing, which would interfere with the movements of the car [when moved over rough ground]."

A story in the December 1940 edition of *The Diner* profiled manufacturing at Silk City. Everett Reynolds Cooper, sales manager, said that diner frames were "built of steel and arc-welded at all joints. It's the same idea as is

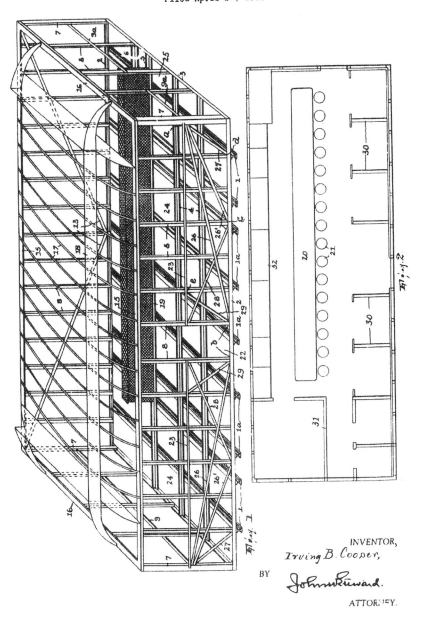

I. B. COOPER 2,145,919

VEHICLE BODY CONSTRUCTION

Filed April 27, 1938

INVENTOR,

Irving B. Cooper,

BY

John Steward.

ATTORNEY.

Patent diagram by Irving Cooper. *Courtesy of Les Cooper.*

used in building the new streamlined railroad cars or the latest design in shipbuilding." During World War II, diner production was interrupted, and the factory was reconfigured to make industrial crates used to ship Curtiss-Wright airport engines.

Sales brochures from the 1950s indicated that Silk City offered three standard sizes of diner cars: forty by sixteen feet, forty-five by sixteen feet and fifty by sixteen feet. Taking a cue from its experience in vehicle production, diner manufacturing techniques were engineered to minimize variation and reduce cost while maximizing consistent, efficient workflow. Silk City also underlined its capabilities in metalworking and steel welding and espoused the virtues of modular construction and integrated food-preparation components such as refrigerators, steam tables, grills, coffee urns and work benches.

Patriarch Everett Abbott Cooper died at age ninety-two on January 4, 1953, at his home on Derron Avenue in Paterson, as reported in the January 5, 1953 edition of the *Paterson Evening News*. The obituary stated that Cooper was born near Suffern on May 11, 1860, and that his family was among the early Dutch settlers of Rockland County, New York. He was president of the Village of Suffern and served as a delegate to state and national Republican conventions.

In the mid-1950s, the company drafted a form letter for prospective customers, predicting that by 1960 the nation's restaurant business would be a $20 billion market. The letter identified lifestyle trends for the burgeoning American middle class:

> *Twenty five out of 100 meals served in this country are served outside the home. Every year more people are eating out. There is an actual shortage of eating places today. Working people are earning more money, have shorter hours and more time for relaxation, sports and travel. Today people are on the go. They are restless. They eat more than ever because their energy requires more food. New roads are being built for the millions of cars that are going to be needed in the near future. These roads require eating places and many new diner owners will get their share of the national travel dollar. More industries are moving into rural areas near good highways and with higher pay workers do not take their lunches. They eat in diners or restaurants.*

The letter ended by inviting those interested in the pitch to call the sales team and "reverse the charges."

The sale of Silk City diners encompassed the life and career of John Grinwis, who was born on Madison Avenue in Paterson in December

1902. At age fourteen, he got a part-time job at the Paterson Vehicle Company, sweeping the factory floor. He remained with the company most of his adult life, becoming the vice-president of sales for Silk City Diners. His daughter, Marilyn Grinwis Gray, said that his strong work ethic came from his Dutch roots. John's father, Cornelius Grinwis, was born in Ouddorp, a town on a peninsula in southern Holland. In the early 1900s, Paterson had many Dutch families. "It was a close-knit community," she said during a 2013 interview. "There were many old-time Dutchmen who worked at the Paterson Vehicle Company."

Marilyn described her dad as a dedicated salesman who kept in touch with his clients. "He was very proud when his customers were successful. He worked with them to pick the best site for a diner." She said that he finalized the sale of the original Tick Tock Diner in Clifton in 1952 and was pleased when it became a popular establishment. "They picked a good spot for the diner. People enjoyed going there. That made him happy." She said that her dad often took the family out to eat at diners. "We'd always go to a different one," Marilyn said. "If it wasn't dinner, then we went to a diner for coffee and dessert."

A company memo to "all directors or their agents" on April 20, 1964, stated that due to the death of its president, Abbott E. Cooper, the Paterson Vehicle Company decided to "discontinued the manufacture" of its Silk City Diners. An obituary in the March 28, 1964 edition of the *Paterson Evening News* reported that Cooper, age seventy-four, died at his home in Ridgewood on March 26. The memo went on to say that the company's stockholders "feel that they would like to show some consideration to Otto C. Pehle [the shop foreman] and John Grinwis due to their long and faithful connection with the company." The two remaining Cooper family executives (William and Fred) were in their early seventies and no longer wanted to pursue the diner business. The memo spelled out plans to start a new Silk City Diner Corporation, with Pehle and Grinwis renting the Paterson factory, assuming insurance, leasing and financial responsibilities and purchasing the remaining inventory on the factory floor: two diners (serial nos. 8471 and 5471) for $52,400.

In a letter to company executives dated June 17, 1964, Pehle and Grinwis stated that they were "in the process of trying to arrange the necessary financing and awaiting the reply of accountants...It is our hope that a satisfactory arrangement can be arrived at for all concerned." However, the transaction was never finalized, as Pehle and Grinwis were unable to secure the financing to move forward with the plans for the new Silk City concern.

Roadside Diner, Wall Township. *Photo by M. Gabriele.*

As a result, stockholders met on December 28, 1965, and the Paterson Vehicle Company initiated liquidation proceedings, which were completed in January 1966. Marilyn said that her father was deeply disappointed when the deal fell through, as he had hoped to continue in the diner business with Pehle. John Grinwis died in Paterson on October 27, 1974.

Vintage Silk City diners operating today include the Roadside Diner in Wall and the Salem Oak Diner in Salem. In a tale of rebirth, a June 9, 2013 article published by the *New Hampshire Union Leader* reported that a 1947 Silk City car, salvaged by Diversified Diners, was transported to Rindge, New Hampshire. A local businessman purchased the diner with plans to open it at the intersection of Routes 119 and 202.

HOMETOWN HEARTSTRINGS

Mountain View was the name of Henry Strys's hometown. It also became the name of his company. An obituary in the November 9, 1972 edition of the *New Jersey Herald* said that he was born on October 27, 1909, in the Mountain View section of Wayne and died on November 8, 1972.

Strys and Les Daniel (aforementioned) were kindred spirits who formed an alliance in 1939 to launch Mountain View Diners, which was located on the

This postcard shows the West Hoboken Transfer Station and its web of trolley tracks. The card's image, which dates to 1908, features Jack's Quick Lunch, a lunch cart that predated the O'Mahony wagon purchased by Michael Griffin. *From the collection of M. Gabriele.*

Prout's Diner, Sussex. *Courtesy of Larry Cultrera.*

The White Crystal Diner being rebuilt at Diversified Diners, Cleveland. *Courtesy of Steve Harwin.*

Rosie's Diner
in Rockford,
Michigan. *Courtesy
of Jerry Berta.*

Arlington Diner,
North Arlington.
Photo by M. Gabriele.

The Tick Tock
rooftop sign. *Photo
by M. Gabriele.*

Silver Moon Diner, Baltimore—the last Kullman diner. *Courtesy of J.M. Giordano.*

Red Hawk Diner, Montclair State University. *Photo by M. Gabriele.*

Bendix Diner, Hasbrouck Heights. *Photo by M. Gabriele.*

Road Island Diner, Oakley, Utah. *Courtesy of Doung Hoang.*

Tony's Freehold Grill, Freehold. *Photo by M. Gabriele.*

Miss America, Jersey City. *Photo by M. Gabriele.*

Above: Hot turkey platter, Tick Tock Diner. *Photo by M. Gabriele.*

Below: Greek salad with spinach pies, Tick Tock Diner. *Photo by M. Gabriele.*

Opposite, top: Lido Diner, Springfield. *Courtesy of Don and Newly Preziosi.*

Opposite, middle: Café des Cascadeurs (formerly the Excellent Diner). *Courtesy of Elaine Swingle.*

Opposite, bottom: Circle Diner, Flemington Circle, circa 1955. *Courtesy of Don and Newly Preziosi.*

Chocolate crepes, Tick Tock Diner. *Photo by M. Gabriele.*

Breakfast at the Bendix Diner, October 2012. *Photo by M. Gabriele.*

Taco salad with Buffalo chicken strips, Nevada Diner, Bloomfield. *Photo by M. Gabriele.*

The Colonial Diner on Orient Way in Lyndhurst, which opened in 1950, shows the signature exterior design feature of diners built by Mountain View: the stainless steel "cow catcher" corner. Gus Gremanis and his family purchased the Colonial Diner in 1985 and renovated the place three years ago. *Photo by M. Gabriele.*

Key City Diner, Phillipsburg. *Photo by M. Gabriele.*

Newark/Pompton Turnpike (Route 23) in the Singac section of Little Falls. Both had a methodical, scientific approach to manufacturing. An article in the August 1941 edition of *The Diner* offered a profile of the partners. Daniel had been a foreman with existing diner builders going back to the mid-1920s. "I've worked for a lot of big companies. I think I've learned how to build a diner more from watching other people's errors than seeing what was done right," he stated in the feature. Strys was an experienced contractor and builder. He reconditioned his first diner in 1938, according to the *Diner* article. He and Daniel pooled their wisdom and manufacturing philosophy in the company's slogan: "A Mountain View Diner Will Last a Lifetime."

At least two Mountain View diners are listed on the National Register of Historic Places. The 29 Diner, located on Route 29 in Fairfax, Virginia, made the register in 1992. An article posted on ConnectionNewspapers.com ("The Taste of Nostalgia") said that the 29 Diner was opened on July 20, 1947. An essay on the 29 Diner website described the establishment as "a rare fragment of early-20th century roadside architecture."

Davies' Chuck Wagon Diner in Lakewood, Colorado, was placed on the National Register in 1997. A story posted online (www.davieschuckwagon.com) noted that William Lyman Davies was the original owner of the diner. Davies had worked as a supervisor for Walgreens drugstore restaurants for more than twenty years, a job that involved a considerable amount of travel throughout the United States. His dream was to open his own eatery in Colorado—a stainless steel diner, like the ones he admired during his stays in the Northeast.

"In 1956, Lyman Davies was looking for a diner company to his liking and after much research he ordered from Mountain View a modified show diner, similar to the show diner used in the 37th National Restaurant Show in Chicago," the website story reported. The Mountain View diner, no. 516, arrived by rail in Denver in 1957. Davies spent $92,000 for the diner and $3,600 for the shipping fee, in addition to the cost of the land. The diner opened in June 21, 1957, and offered twenty-four-hour service, and according to the article, it was an immediate hit. "Within two weeks the place was packed, especially at lunch time, when lines formed around the building."

The diner built for Davies was one of the final bookings for Mountain View. Gutman wrote that the company "attempted to go public in June 1956 and was out of business shortly thereafter." One reason for the company's demise involved the overall downturn in the diner market. In addition, the company was burdened with a large inventory of used and repossessed diners that were deemed overpriced and couldn't be resold.

Made by Manno

The first thing you notice is the zigzag. The Manno Dining Car Company built the Americana Diner, circa 1950, which features the dazzling "zigzag" or "folded-plate" outdoor window frames along with interior granite counters and decorative neon lights. The terrazzo floor of the West Orange diner's vestibule displays the letters "TC," which stand for the eatery's original name, the Tory Corner Diner. According to information on the Revolutionary War New Jersey and West Orange History websites, the intersection of Washington and Main Streets is a section of town still known as "Tory Corner" (not far from the Americana Diner)—a site where the Tories or Loyalists would gather for rallies during the 1770s. Prior to the name Americana Diner, the eatery was known as the West Orange Pancake House and Diner and still features pancakes on its menu.

Another Manno beauty is the Broadway Diner in Red Bank, which has a stylish exterior adorned with glass brick, stainless steel and neon lights. Inside the diner, a framed newspaper clipping of the September 20, 1959 edition of the *Asbury Park Press* states that the eatery, purchased for $125,000, was built in Belleville and delivered in sections during an all-night convoy by tractor-trailer trucks (via police escort) on the morning of August 18, 1959. The first section—the main body of the diner—measured fifty-three feet

Americana Diner, West Orange. *Photo by M. Gabriele.*

Broadway Diner, Red Bank. *Photo by M. Gabriele.*

long and eighteen feet wide. The Broadway replaced the Palace Diner, a barrel-roofed O'Mahony car that was installed in 1941. Prior to the Palace and Broadway, there was a YMCA on the Monmouth Street lot.

Ralph Manno, who worked at Kullman for twenty-two years, founded the company in 1949 with Vincent Giannotti, according to Gutman. Manno, which also had a plant in Fairfield, closed its shop in 1978. Other examples of Manno eateries in northern New Jersey are Jay's Grill on Bloomfield Avenue, Bloomfield, and Main Line Pizza, at the intersection of East Main Street and Van Ness Avenue, Little Falls.

RARE SURVIVORS

By 1925, Jerry O'Mahony Inc. had outgrown four different Bayonne locations, and the company moved to 977–991 West Grand Street in Elizabeth, a thirty-five-thousand-square-foot manufacturing plant that was adjacent to the Jersey Central Railroad. The year 1925 was also when Jerry and his family moved to an elegant home, which he had built at 265 East Dudley Avenue in Westfield. In November 1927, the company unveiled its Monarch line of diners. There were six models in the series, measuring forty to forty-five feet in length, with a variety of table and counter configurations. The series featured mahogany interior wood, Gothic-style windows, oxidized silver fixtures and ceramic tile floors.

There are few 1920s-era O'Mahony diners still in service. One is Dan's Diner, located on Route 203 in Spencertown, New York, a 1925 car that was restored by local businessman Dan Rundell and opened in 2008. Cultrera, writing in his "Diner Hotline" blog, said that the diner previously was known as Moe's Diner and the Durham Diner in Durham, Connecticut. In 1993, Rundell purchased the structure from a Connecticut scrapyard and moved it to Columbia County, New York.

Another early model is Skee's Diner (O'Mahony car no. 562) in Torrington, Connecticut. The Torrington Historic Preservation Trust assumed ownership of Skee's on July 1, 2013, with plans to restore the eatery. Northwest Connecticut's chamber of commerce, which acquired the diner in 2009, gifted Skee's to the preservation trust. Mark McEachern, treasurer, and Edward Cook, president—both members of the preservation trust's executive board—are heading the renovation project.

Skee's Diner, Torrington, Connecticut. *Courtesy of Mark McEachern.*

Skee's was added to the National Park Service's National Register of Historic Places on September 6, 2002. The Statement of Significance section of the National Register application explained:

> *Skee's Diner is an important example of the barrel-roof diner in Connecticut. The structure is significant for its association with Jerry O'Mahony, Inc. of Bayonne and Elizabeth, New Jersey. Skee's is the earliest known surviving O'Mahony diner in the state and displays an impressive level of integrity from its original date of manufacture. Alterations to the structure…reflect noteworthy trends in the design and function of diners over time. The property has local historical significance as a resource, which recalls the early years of Torrington's automobile-related commercial development.*

Eleven feet wide and thirty feet long, Skee's is constructed with a wood frame that utilizes channel iron and sheet metal panels. The interior has sixteen stools (originally there were eighteen), a tan-colored marble counter, green and black ceramic floor tiles, a mahogany interior and stainless steel trim and display cases.

McEachern said that the preservation trust's research indicates that the diner most likely was built in the late 1920s or possibly 1930. A timeline constructed by the organization and posted on the Skee's website (www.skeesdiner.org) notes that the diner originally was shipped to southern Connecticut (possibly the Old Saybrook area) from New Jersey about eighty years ago. In 1945, Rudolph (Rudy) Cielke, a restaurant owner, bought the diner and moved it to Torrington. On August 31, 1945, Cielke signed a land lease and received a permit to dig a foundation for the eatery at the northwest corner of North Elm and Main Street (Lawrence Square). The diner was installed at that location, and based on town documents, it's believed that Cielke, along with two associates, Tom Ryan and John Miran, briefly ran the establishment in late 1945 as "Rudy's Diner."

Anthony Cisowski, a World War II veteran, purchased the diner from Cielke on February 11, 1946. Cisowski and his brother, Edmund, took charge of the business and hired Stanley "Stash" Smigel as the cook. On October 7, 1946, Rudy's Diner officially changed its name to "Skee's," which was Cisowski's nickname during his time in the navy.

The National Register document notes that Skee's operated twenty-one hours a day and offered a menu that included pot roast, swordfish, sauerkraut and sausage and goulash. Business boomed in the late 1940s (the document quoted Cisowski as saying, "The seats never got cold"). The Cisowski brothers ran the business until 1975, when they sold the diner to Judith A. Belmonte. During the 1980s and 1990s, Skee's went through a series of ownership changes until finally closing in 2001. In the ensuing years, there was an assortment of proposals put forth to relocate the venerable structure.

On April 13, 2013, Skee's—weighing in at twenty-eight thousand pounds—was moved to a warehouse from its Lawrence Square site to begin the restoration work. McEachern, quoted in the March 8, 2013 edition of the Torrington-based *Register Citizen* newspaper, said that the preservation trust, working with the Torrington Historical Society, will keep Skee's in Torrington, with a goal of restoring the diner to "its former glory" as an operational restaurant.

THE YEAR 1928 was a banner one for O'Mahony as the company registered sales of $1.5 million. Business was strong, and the expanded accommodations of the Elizabeth facility served as a springboard for a prosperous decade of diner production during the 1930s. Three jewels from this vintage era still thriving today are the Summit Diner, Summit; the Road Island Diner, Oakley, Utah; and Mickey's Diner, St. Paul, Minnesota.

The three O'Mahony survivors are examples of the golden age for New Jersey diner builders, when many manufacturers prominently incorporated the aerodynamic curves and extended horizontal lines that were characteristic of the Streamline Moderne industrial design movement. Materials such as stainless steel, glass bricks, Formica and Bakelite were in vogue. "These were the years when diners became bright, welcoming beacons along the nation's highways and streets," Marhoefer wrote. The website art.nuvvo.com defines Streamline Moderne as a late branch (1930–50) of Art Deco. The design style captures the "growth of speed, travel and technology in the 1930s. The architectural style of buildings [especially diners] looked similar to that of the new technology—automobiles, trains, ocean ships and airplanes. It reflected the law of aerodynamics in architectural form."

An August 31, 2011 article in the *Independent Press* (nj.com) reported that Summit's downtown shopping district, which includes the Summit Diner, had earned a spot on the National Register of Historic Places in July 2011. The Union County town's application for the National Register stated that the Summit Diner, built in 1938, "is one of the most distinctive in New Jersey, a state known for its diner culture. The existing Jerry O'Mahony Company dining car was erected on the site of an earlier diner on Union Place. The Streamline Moderne–style building is an excellent example of its type and retains a high level of architectural integrity."

Summit Diner, Summit. *Photo by M. Gabriele.*

The Road Island Diner made the National Register in August 2009. According to information posted on the Utah State History website, O'Mahony dining car no. 1107 was custom-built for exhibition at the 1939 World's Fair in New York. After the fair, it went to Fall River, Massachusetts, and became McDermott's Diner. In 1953, it was moved to Route 138 in Middletown, Rhode Island, and renamed Tommy's Deluxe Diner—a fixture in the Ocean State for fifty-three years. Entrepreneur Keith Walker purchased the diner in 2006, moved it to Utah and then restored and opened it as the Road Island Diner in July 2008.

Three years ago, Artair (Petey) Cameron was driving on Route 32 in Utah, passing through Oakley and feeling hungry and in need of a cup of coffee. He spied the glistening Road Island Diner in the distance—a place unlike anything he had ever seen. And although it wasn't in his travel plans that day, he knew that he had reached his destination. It turned out to be a journey that changed his life. "I showed up one day for a cup of coffee and never left," he said. "I guess that was one hell of a cup of coffee." Since then, he has come to be known as "Petey" and is the "lead server" at the Road Island Diner (maitre d' is much too fancy a title, he insisted). He wears a red bow tie, knows how to treat his customers right and takes care of business. Born in Utah, Petey was raised in Edinburgh, Scotland, by his grandparents, served in the U.S. Marine Corps, spent several years working in the restaurant business and eventually returned to the Beehive State.

"People come here, and they say it feels like home," he said. "When I see my regular customers pull into the parking lot, I place their order before they walk in the door. We also get tourists passing through who've never been here before. Now, if it's your first time here, I *will* sit down with you, and we'll have a good time. We have a good time here every day."

The diner serves classic American comfort food, a menu that features macaroni and cheese, meatloaf and homemade desserts. There's also a barbecue menu, as the diner has an outdoor smoker. The Road Island Diner has eighteen stools and fourteen booths plus outdoor patio seating during the spring and summer months. There's also a basement banquet room. The diner has been restored to its pristine 1939 World's Fair condition. What possessed Keith Walker to take on this venture and haul the diner more than two thousand miles to Utah from Rhode Island? "Mr. Walker is a big fan of Americana and nostalgia," Petey said. "It all comes from his heart."

The National Register registration form explained the Road Island Diner's design and cultural significance:

> *Dining Car No. 1107 is a one-of-kind, custom-built model that marks the pivot point in diner design for the O'Mahony Company and represents the transition from the standard pre-war design of diners to the post-War direction of the mobile diner industry. Just a few years prior to World War II, the O'Mahony Company began adding rounded corners and applying steel/porcelain bands to the exterior of its traditional monitor-roof dining car models. The design of Dining Car No. 1107 broke with the company's tradition, with the emphasis on alternating bands of stainless steel and porcelain that more fully realized the design objectives of the Streamlined Moderne movement, invoking the sleekness of the stainless steel rail cars of the period. In size and materials, Dining Car No. 1107 was the prototype for the O'Mahony dining cars of the late 1940s and early 1950s.*

Mickey's Diner was installed on the National Register in February 1983. Marhoefer, who resided in Minneapolis in 1982, recalled reading a newspaper article that said that the Minnesota Historic Commission was reviewing several properties being considered for nomination to the National Register—Mickey's Diner being one of them. But she learned that because the eatery was not yet fifty years old, it didn't qualify for the register. Looking to help the cause, Marhoefer attended the hearing, spelled out the significance of the diner and urged the state commission to make an exception for Mickey's. She was pleased when the commission voted six to two to suspend the fifty-year rule in favor of Mickey's.

Mickey's Diner, St. Paul, Minnesota, 1982. *Courtesy of the Minnesota Historical Society Library.*

Eric Mattson, the son of the diner's original owner, Bert Mattson, told Marhoefer the importance of being listed on the National Register. Located in downtown St. Paul on Ninth Street, the diner is adjacent to a popular park, bus station and convention center. Prior to achieving "historic" status, Eric Mattson said that the city had planned to move Mickey's from its familiar, plum location.

Bert Mattson and Mickey Crimmons purchased the diner in 1939 at the Chicago Restaurant Show for $30,000. Mattson eventually bought out Crimmons's share of the business but retained his partner's name for the diner. Today, Eric Mattson's daughter and son, Melissa and Bert, represent the Mattson family's third generation running the diner. They've continued the seventy-four-year tradition of keeping the diner open twenty-four hours a day, seven days a week.

The National Register's nomination form for Mickey's Diner, dated February 24, 1983, and provided by the State Historic Preservation Office/Minnesota Historical Society, described the eatery's

> *historic importance as a beloved, long-standing and unique social institution, which is a landmark in downtown Saint Paul; an unaltered, classic railroad-car-inspired, American blue-collar diner, which is an excellent example of streamlined architecture. Mickey's Diner was prefabricated in Elizabeth, New Jersey, in 1937...and shipped to Saint Paul by rail and installed on*

its present site in 1939. It has remained in continuous operation since then, and is a popular local establishment. At a time when most such businesses have been replaced by fast food chains and franchises…Mickey's is a rare survivor of the 1930s and 1940s era, when manufactured diners were commonplace in the American landscape.

The description section of the nomination form noted that the diner's exterior "features yellow and red porcelain/steel panels, plate glass windows in a horizontal band and divided by fluted chrome strips, [Art] Deco–style lettering, and a roof topped by a projecting upright sign, illuminated with neon and a ribbon of light-bulb edging. The interior of the building has stainless steel grills and fixtures with a sunburst motif, booths and stools to accommodate 36 customers, and wall surfaces sheathed in mahogany paneling and smoked-glass mirrors."

By the 1940s, manufacturers had defined the economic science and metrics of the diner business, an array of marketing statistics compiled and analyzed over the years to entice potential customers. The 1941 O'Mahony catalogue's marketing literature declared that "a modern Jerry O'Mahony dining car in an average location will serve between 500 and 700 customers per day…Study these figures carefully; see for yourself how you can earn $5,000 to $10,000 a year." In addition, a modern O'Mahony diner was built to be user friendly. "Four connections are all that are necessary. When the gas, water, electricity and sewer are connected, your diner is ready for use. Every individual item of equipment selected for use is chosen only after extensive research for durability and efficiency."

Internal company documents from 1941 recorded the sale of fifty-one diners with a trade-in allowance for seventeen. Following 1941, with United States engaged World War II, diner production in Elizabeth was put on hold, and the government contracted the O'Mahony plant to produce truck bodies for the army, redeploying the company's manufacturing expertise. After the war, O'Mahony began filling back orders.

TIME TO RETIRE

In the fall of 1950, Jerry O'Mahony retired from the diner business and sold the company. He and his wife, Kate, moved to North Miami, Florida. Marhoefer referenced a document, dated September 3, 1950, that illustrates the floor plan of the Elizabeth production facility. The drawing most likely was created in preparation for the sale of the business. The diagram shows nine new diners under construction on the factory floor, with an additional two previously owned diners being rebuilt. The plant layout had five bays, one of which was a carpenter shop; a separate warehouse where the two used diners and two new diners were stored; a sheet metal department; a stockroom; offices for engineering and finance; and a loading dock that was adjacent to the railroad line.

The July 1952 edition of *Fortune* magazine reported that O'Mahony had sold the business for $1.3 million to a group of New Jersey investors. A business brief in the June 3, 1953 edition of the *New York Times* reported that the company—still known as Jerry O'Mahony Inc.—acquired Standsteel Corporation, a Long Island–based producer of steel office equipment. Louis F. Camardella was quoted in the article as the company president. Other acquisitions included the Herman Body Company, a St. Louis builder of truck bodies, and Bennel Machine Company Inc., a Brooklyn-based maker of airplane parts. On September 1, 1953, the company installed Carl G. Strandlund as president, with Camardella becoming board chairman.

The *Times*, in a September 23, 1951 article, quoted an O'Mahony spokesman, who said that the diner business was healthy and profitable. The spokesman estimated that there were six thousand diners in the United States (most of which were east of the Mississippi River), serving 2.4 million customers on a daily basis. "The owners [annually] spend $217 million for food and take in $500 million in sales." The article cited the production of a double-car O'Mahony diner, being sold for $105,000, which offered seating to 100 people. Despite its size, the article stated that it was still considered to be a diner "since it is erected in a plant, moved to a site and placed on a foundation, from which it can be moved at any time desired. Because it is movable, it is classified as personal property and not real estate, and is taxed as such."

The O'Mahony expansion and diversification strategy anticipated a strong postwar boom for diners. Car-happy Americans filled with wanderlust were "getting their kicks on Route 66" and elsewhere. A headline for an August 31, 1952 *Times* article said that "many new diners are due to appear—manufacturers eye Western sites to meet the demand of prospective owners." The story reported that diners, well established as a "big business" in the East, are expected to "spread westward like a prairie fire," with "operators begging for their share of this roadside business."

New Jersey's diner manufacturing sector was in search of a lucrative "export" market—states west of the Mississippi. In addition to O'Mahony, the article stated that other Garden State diner builders—Paramount, Kullman, Mountain View and the Silk City unit of the Paterson Vehicle Company—were also mulling plans to open production facilities in the Midwest. "There are vast, untapped markets," Camardella told the *Times*, referring to western regions. "It's not a question of sales any more, but of capacity and production." According to Camardella, the Elizabeth plant was "under an avalanche of orders. We can make only 30 diners a year with our present facilities. We could easily sell three or four times as many."

However, ambitious plans for a western expansion did not pan out. "Jerry O'Mahony Inc. was mortgaged to the hilt and struggled to stay in business," Gutman wrote. The May 10, 1956 edition of the *Elizabeth Daily Journal* reported that the company released its sixty employees and was closing. The story said that the company, saddled with its acquisition debt, had undergone reorganizations following the change in ownership. "The firm acquired several subsidiaries and at one time was prepared to manufacture diners in its St. Louis plant, but financial difficulties ensued."

The *Daily Journal* story quoted Joseph A. Montano, vice-president and general manager of O'Mahony, who revealed that there were "four incomplete diners" on the factory floor of the shuttered company. Montano and two other partners—who founded the short-lived Mahony Diners Inc. in Kearny—purchased at least one of the unfinished diners, possibly all four. Montano, in a handwritten letter to Marhoefer dated September 21, 2005, recalled that he and his associates acquired one "partially constructed" car from the Elizabeth plant. It was finished and shipped to Scranton, Pennsylvania.

The last complete diner to come off the O'Mahony production line in Elizabeth was Bosko's Diner, which was shipped to South River in 1955, according to the 1980 book *Diners of the Northeast* by Donald Kaplan and Alan Bellink. Carole Bosko, interviewed in May 2013, said that her father, John, and a partner, Ben Turbach, went into business in 1945, right after her father finished his stint in the army, serving in Europe during World War II. There was an existing eatery at 122 Causeway, and the partners renamed the establishment B&T Diner. Ten years later, Bosko and Turbach purchased their new O'Mahony diner. Carol Bosko said that her father bought out Turbach not long after the new diner was installed, but the B&T name stuck with the South River locals.

Carole Bosko, who graduated from South River High School in 1959, has fond memories of her father's place, saying that it was a favorite hangout for her classmates, especially after high school dances. She said that her father retired from the business in early 1983 and died in September of that year. The diner changed hands over the years, and a remodeled version of the structure sits idle at 115 Causeway.

How the West Wasn't Won

Why did the western expansion strategy fail? Andrew Hurley, PhD, a history professor at the University of Missouri–St. Louis and the author of the book *Diners, Bowling Alleys, and Trailer Parks: Chasing the American Dream in Postwar Consumer Culture* (published in 2001), said that O'Mahony and Mountain View were two New Jersey diner builders that made a serious attempt to gain a foothold in the West. Hurley said that their efforts fell short due to the stiff competition they encountered from drive-ins, highway truck stops and California "coffee shops." These eateries had their own distinct histories and developed on tracks parallel with diners, reflecting the culture of the western and southern regions of America.

Diners found it hard to penetrate the western frontier because they, quite literally, didn't fit into this landscape as a dining concept for the emerging, postwar middle class, according to Hurley. "There was strong push back to the 'East Coast, stainless steel look' of diners. It carried a negative reputation." In his book, Hurley wrote that it was unusual to find a prefabricated diner anywhere between the Mississippi River and the Pacific Ocean. "Overly adventurous [diner] operators and builders ran into trouble when they tried to place diners in unfamiliar territory. In the nation's interior, many communities frowned on what they considered an intrusion from the East Coast."

Hurley said that perhaps diners might have been embraced more enthusiastically had it not been for the popularity of another type of eatery: the drive-in. During the 1950s, drive-ins were soaring in the Midwest and South, and some evolved into a franchise chain or fast-food restaurant business, such as Bob's Big Boy and McDonald's. "Diners never adapted that business model," he said.

Drive-ins developed their own distinctive Streamline Moderne architectural style to lure customers from the road. Jim Heimann, in his 1996 book *Car Hops and Curb Service: A History of American Drive-In Restaurants 1920–1950*, wrote that the drive-in was born on the Dallas/Fort Worth Highway, outside of Dallas, Texas, in September 1921 with the launch of the Pig Stands Company Inc. Heimann wrote that this was the first restaurant specifically designed to serve meals to motorists in their cars. The drive-in concept quickly took root in the Lone Star State and then migrated to California. Another well-established restaurant genre that fended off the diner intrusion was the California coffee shop, which had similarities to the social niche of diners. Meanwhile, highway truck stops, grills and cafés had mystiques and legends all their own.

Despite the unsuccessful western migration, Hurley paid tribute to the historical significance of diners and their contribution to the postwar consumer culture. "The diner was only one among many institutions that guided upwardly mobile Americans into the unsettling and tantalizing world of consumer affluence after World War II."

A Brooklyn Dodgers Fan

Company archivist Barbara Marhoefer described Jerry O'Mahony as an outgoing, loving grandfather, saying that he set up trust funds for his nineteen grandchildren. "Many of us went to college on that money." He also was "secretly generous" to friends who faced serious medical problems or financial hardships.

"Jerry and I were avid Brooklyn Dodger fans," she recalled. "He took me to my first baseball game to see the marvelous Jackie Robinson at Ebbets Field. Jerry loved playing golf and cards. He loved cars, particularly Cadillacs, but never bought one [he drove a small Chrysler coupe]. He felt it wasn't fitting for him to have a Cadillac, but he always went outside the plant to admire a customer's new Cadillac."

As a little girl, Marhoefer often accompanied her grandparents on field trips to visit O'Mahony diners. The meal usually was lunch, and Jerry typically ordered broiled fish. "My mother told me that, on their honeymoon, Jerry and Kate left Bayonne and drove to East Orange to inspect a site for a diner." She said that her grandparents often traveled together and enjoyed four world cruises. Although successful in business, Marhoefer revealed that Jerry had only a limited formal education. "He left school in the fourth grade and went to work to help support his family. My mother said that when she was in elementary school, Jerry sat with her at their kitchen table in the evenings and studied her textbooks, practicing his figures in rows and rows of addition, subtraction, multiplication and division."

Left: Jerry O'Mahony. *Courtesy of Barbara McGeary Marhoefer.*

Below: Harris Diner, East Orange. *Photo by M. Gabriele.*

The spelling of the company and family name has become a curiosity over the years. Marhoefer said that Jerry's father was Michael Mahoney. For most family members in Bayonne, the preferred spelling of the name was O'Mahony. Outside of the diner business, Jerry signed his last name as O'Mahoney. When Jerry and his family moved to Westfield in 1925, the family name was Mahoney. Marhoefer said that older aunts and uncles speculated that the "O" in the name was used to accentuate the family's Irish ancestry. She also cited feedback from author and Bayonne historian Middleton, who said that it was common for families in the early 1900s to tinker with the spelling of surnames.

Jeremiah O'Mahony died on March 3, 1969, at the age of eighty-nine. He suffered a heart attack and succumbed at Overlook Hospital in Summit. His beloved wife, Kate, died on May 7, 1967. John J. Hanf, the carpenter who helped Jerry develop the Bayonne lunch wagon business, died on March 4, 1950, at the age of seventy-one. He worked for the company for nearly thirty years and retired in 1940.

"My grandfather was a pioneer who transformed the diner industry," Marhoefer said, describing his legacy in the Garden State. "He owned and operated three chains of his own diners and was constantly improving diner design. He built more than 2,100 diners over thirty-eight years and helped make the diner the beloved American icon we know today." In addition to the Summit Diner, classic O'Mahony diners can still be found throughout the Garden State: the Harris Diner, East Orange; Tony's Freehold Grill, Freehold; Miss American Diner, Jersey City; Royal Diner, Washington; and 25 Burgers Diner (the former Branchburg Diner), Branchburg.

Part IV

Time Made Visible

TEMPLES OF A LOST CIVILIZATION

There is a cadre of historians, craftsmen, writers, bloggers and artists committed to the preservation of diners in New Jersey and beyond. Their passion for diners and the Americana spirit is expressed in many ways, from books to websites to hands-on restoration. They are loyal customers and astute observers who themselves have become part of diner history. Their efforts have created an awareness for the greater appreciation of diners—their value as a cultural institution, as an expression of American industrial design and as a popular field of nostalgia. It's a noble pursuit, and as members of the intelligentsia, each brings a different perspective to the study of diners. Some have made it their life's work.

"Richard J.S. Gutman, recently graduated from Cornell's College of Architecture, Art and Planning…[he] is the important architectural historian of the diner." So wrote *The New Yorker* magazine in its September 30, 1972 edition. The architectural and cultural history of diners has become Gutman's passion and profession as he serves as the director and curator of the Culinary Arts Museum at Johnson & Wales University in Providence, Rhode Island, which houses a vast collection of diner literature, photos, authentic artifacts and memorabilia.

Gutman, twenty-three at the time, was featured in *The New Yorker*'s coverage of an exhibition titled Objects for Preparing Food, which was held in Manhattan's Museum of Contemporary Crafts. The exhibit, along with the magazine coverage, launched his career as the go-to authority on American diners. Gutman's work in the ensuing years, especially his book *American Diner*, generated interest in diner culture. As the diner capital of America, New Jersey maintains a special place in his heart. Working at the university museum in Providence, Gutman doesn't have to go far to get a daily dose of Jersey-built diner ambiance. The distance is precisely 1.5 miles due north. His favorite lunch haunt is the Seaplane Diner, a sparkling 1952 stainless steel O'Mahony.

The preservation of golden-age diners can be a "difficult road to travel," Gutman admitted. "There are many people who feel passionately about diners, but not everyone in a community may buy into a restoration project, especially if the goal is to have a diner used for its original purpose. It takes a lot of money to renovate and run a vintage diner." He remains a strong advocate for preserving classic diners.

During the 1980s and 1990s, diner consciousness became widespread as part of the retro/nostalgia craze to resurrect treasured images of American culture. Gutman said that the interest in diners is similar to the enthusiasm people feel for preserving and showcasing classic cars. He's convinced that diners will remain part of the American landscape. Some classic relics will survive and epitomize the style and romance of an older era, he said, drawing a comparison to beloved landmarks such as the White Horse Tavern in Newport, Rhode Island, or McSorley's Old Ale House in New York City.

"Diners will always have an appeal," he said. "They provide good food and fast service at a good value. They attract a diverse mixture of people. Just like in the past, they will evolve and reflect popular culture. They will be efficient, comfortable places where people will want to gather. The American diner will continue to have its own niche, but with many new variations. Diners in the twenty-first century will continue to serve the type of food that people will want to eat," he predicted, noting the ethnic influences of Hispanic and Asian cultures, as well as the preference for vegetarian fare, local foods and meals with healthier choices. He's also encouraged to see a "full-circle" moment unfolding: a new generation of free-spirited people who operate modern, motorized lunch wagons (or food trucks). The February 2013 edition of *New Jersey Monthly* posted a list of these food trucks ("Moveable Feasts") that offer exotic, homemade cuisine. These offbeat entrepreneurs are worthy descendants of the original lunch wagon pioneers.

STAR-LEDGER FEATURE writer and author Peter Genovese, in his "Jersey's Best Diners" cover story in the August 2013 edition of *Inside Jersey* magazine, estimated that there are six hundred diners in the Garden State (a higher number than Garbin's count, based on a more inclusive calculus). Genovese, who published the book *Jersey Diners* in 1996, no doubt has logged more Jersey diner miles and meals than anyone. Most recently, for his magazine article, he drove 2,827 miles through all twenty-one counties, visiting fifty-five diners in eleven days. "There are more diners here than in any other state," he wrote. "Every Jerseyan, it seems, has a favorite diner, and good luck trying to convince someone yours is better. Jerseyans don't agree on much, and when it comes to food, even less so. But in the diner capital of the world, debating where you can get the best breakfast or burgers or salads or desserts is always tasty food for thought."

Born in Trenton, Genovese became a raconteur of the road early on in his journalism career, enamored of the folksy kitsch and sublime Americana oddities that he observed during his travels throughout the state. In the 1980s, his morning breakfast routine usually took him to the Lorraine Diner on Route 1 in South Brunswick, which has since been removed and replaced by a McDonald's. He said that Route 130, which opened in the late 1920s and runs north–south from North Brunswick to Deepwater—just over eighty-three miles as the crow flies—has more diners (twenty-six) than any other Garden State highway. "It's an old urban corridor," he said. "It has more of everything."

Landmarks on Route 130 include Mastoris Diner and Restaurant in Bordentown and the Americana Diner in East Windsor. Mary Corcodilos—her family opened the Hightstown Diner in 1927—married Nick Mastoris in 1941. As recorded in her online memoir, Mary and Nick, along with a business partner, purchased property in Bordentown in 1959 near the intersection of Routes 130 and 206 and opened an eatery, which evolved into today's Mastoris. The 350-seat Americana was rated as the "best diner" in Genovese's *Inside Jersey* feature. A sidebar to the article indicated that, on average, the Americana welcomes twelve thousand customers per week.

Referencing the copious notes compiled for his magazine article, critiquing the finer points of food, service and ambiance, Genovese said that he has not one but many favorite Jersey diners—a magnanimous view that reflects the expansive range of his work. "Big or small, good or bad, all diners go to heaven," he declared.

THE GOAL FOR American photorealist artist John Baeder is to capture the "spirit of place" of quintessential roadside institutions. Baeder, whose 1978 book *Diners* (revised and updated in 1995) is a favorite among Americana connoisseurs, said that he looks to communicate the spirit of his eatery landscapes the same way magic pours out of a jazz musician's horn.

"Capturing 'spirit of place' and the human condition; it's what I try to do in every painting," he said, adding that New Jersey's diverse landscapes resonate with this energy. According to Baeder, spirit of place means executing images that faithfully reflect the quiet dignity of an "everyday" scene and its surroundings. His paintings of diners, food trucks and other roadside attractions typically have a stark, piercing, deceptive simplicity. For Baeder, there is no such thing as an "everyday" scene because no matter how seemingly mundane, there is awe and mystery to be appreciated everywhere. It's all a matter of using his artistic eye to see it, understand it and then translate it as a watercolor or oil painting.

"We often pass by places on our way from here to there. We're always in a hurry. Sometimes we need to stop and take a second look," he said, explaining the aesthetic mindset behind his fascination with diners. "It's a process. Our eyes change; we see things differently and more clearly. Some people, when they're driving, become impatient when they stop at a red light or get stuck in a traffic jam. Whenever I stop, I enjoy it, because there's so much to see."

John Baeder at Max's Grill, Harrison, 1978. *Courtesy of John Baeder.*

An acclaimed American artist for more than forty years, Baeder said that this spirit of place in his older paintings has taken on an even deeper significance. "Some of my early diner paintings, especially the ones from New Jersey, today have more appeal, more meaning for me than when I painted them years ago," he confessed, adding that his artwork has been enhanced by the "patina of time." Baeder is also a stouthearted defender of the Garden State's honor. "I don't like the stigma and the negative stereotypes that people around the country attach to New Jersey. I find it offensive. For me, New Jersey is a vast wonderland. It's a beautiful state."

Born on Christmas Eve 1938 in South Bend, Indiana, Baeder was raised in Atlanta. He came to New York City in the summer of 1964 to continue his career as an art director for advertising agencies. "I grew up in the *Mad Men* era of Madison Avenue," he said, referring to the cable TV show. In the early 1970s, he began a career as a fine artist and began collecting postcards of "main street" American images, which led to his interest in diners. "Coming from Atlanta, diners were something new for me. They were like temples of a lost civilization. I found them cozy and enjoyed eating in them."

WHEN IT COMES to restoring temples of a lost civilization, Cleveland native Steve Harwin has compiled an extensive amount of hands-on experience. Harwin's Diversified Diners business has restored and relocated dozens of New Jersey–built diners since it was established in 1987. Initially, he made a living restoring classic sports cars and motorcycles. While he was traveling in Europe in the early 1980s, several of his European friends started asking him about diners in the United States. They were, Harwin recalled, fascinated by the colorful designs and romance of diners—unlike any eating establishments his friends had encountered in Europe. For them, diners were a foreign curiosity of American culture.

"I was intrigued why they were so interested in diners," Harwin recalled. "There weren't many diners around when I was growing up in Cleveland. At the time, I really didn't know much about diners. But I did appreciate their architecture and design."

After returning to the United States, Harwin was traveling through western Pennsylvania in search of cars and motorcycles. He also was curious to learn more about diners. On his way home to Cleveland, he stopped for a meal in a 1940, all-wood Sterling Streamliner made by the J.B. Judkins Company of Merrimac, Massachusetts. Recalling how American diners captivated his European friends, Harwin inquired and was told that the Streamliner was for sale. Acting on impulse and confident that he could easily transfer the manufacturing skills he gained from refurbishing cars, Harwin thought that rebuilding a diner would be a fun project, an enjoyable diversion from his familiar work.

He was wrong. "It was a disaster and a hell of an education," he confessed during a 2012 phone interview. "I didn't know what I was doing or what I had gotten myself into. Restoring a diner is a lot more complicated than restoring a car."

Not one who gives up easily, Harwin decided to try his hand at rebuilding a second diner. Once again, there were daunting, unforeseen issues. Rather than quit, and perhaps without even realizing it, Harwin was being drawn into a passion for diners. Driven by the challenge, he began to educate himself about diner design and materials. His business gathered traction—one diner restored, one diner sold and then another neglected, forgotten diner was delivered to his 1.5-acre property. "My restorations began to gain notice. There's glamour when it comes to diners." Today, Harwin is a sought-after consultant, has been featured on TV programs and frequently works with private investors, museums and institutions such as Savanna College, Georgia.

He said that there are two common denominators in the restoration of cars and diners: first, beauty is skin deep; and second, you never know how difficult the job will be until you look under the hood—or, in the case of diners, under the roof. The flaws (both obvious and hidden) can be many. Aside from the natural ravages of time, metal oxidation and rotting wood, a sixty-year-old diner must have its utility infrastructure (gas, electric and plumbing) upgraded to meet twenty-first-century building and safety codes. Doors, seats and entry/exit access must accommodate individuals with physical disabilities. Repairing window fixtures is especially problematic. Even after a diner is faithfully restored, getting the approval to transport it to a new location involves dealing with bureaucratic red tape, state by state.

Harwin praised New Jersey diner builders as industrial innovators with an appreciation for classic craftsmanship. "I love old diners. These are structures that merit attention and restoration. They're icons of American culture—well built and historic in nature."

PONDERING QUESTIONS OF how diners fit into New Jersey's landscape of historic preservation, John Hallanan, who serves as president of the Jersey City Landmarks Conservancy, recalled a quote from American author, philosopher and urban theorist Lewis Mumford (1895–1990). "Mumford said great cities are places where time is made visible," Hallanan said. "In other words, you can walk through a city, or even a geographic region, and see different eras and different styles of architecture in the built form. You're able to appreciate a wide range of designs and the diversity of a place. That's what gives great cities a sense of permanence."

For any structure that does merit landmark status, the big challenge is to find a purpose that will sustain its existence. Hallanan pointed out that this utilitarian prerequisite is a clear advantage for diners. "A diner is a perfect example of a useful structure in its existing built form. Diners can be moved to another part of a city, or another part of the state, and still function as a diner."

Diners capture the essence of many eras, he said. As a manufactured product, a diner's "authentic" charm is its design, which reflects the period in which it was constructed. Hallanan said that Jersey City's diverse Millennial/ Generation Y population is fond of all things authentic. "This is a group that's interested in historic diners. They like places with a retro patina. They are more willing to spend their money to support a mom and pop business compared with a national chain." However, the same young consumers who support authenticity are also interested in maintaining a healthier lifestyle, so diners will have to adjust their traditional menus to suit those tastes.

According to Hallanan, Jersey City's two most renowned diner attractions are the Miss America on West Side Avenue, which was manufactured by O'Mahony, and the White Mana on Tonnele Avenue, built by Paramount. The White Mana, displayed at the 1939 World's Fair in New York, was originally heralded as "the diner of the future," Hallanan said. The "other" White Manna Diner (note the different spellings of the biblical bread from heaven) was also built by Paramount and is located in downtown Hackensack on the banks of the Hackensack River.

Jersey City's White Mana celebrated its fiftieth anniversary on June 2, 1996. A proclamation that hangs on its wall, issued by Hudson County executive Robert C. Janiszewski, notes it was purchased by Lou Bridges in 1944 and, two years later, was delivered (in two sections) and installed at the site on Tonnele Avenue (Routes 1 and 9). It was opened on June 2, 1946, and featured carhop service during the 1950s. The White Mana was once part of a five-diner network. Hackensack's White Manna was also opened in 1946. In 1997, the Jersey City Historic Preservation Committee declared the White Mana to be a local landmark.

There are various theories regarding the different spellings (Mana and Manna) of the Jersey City and Hackensack diners. According to information posted on a website from New Jersey City University (NJCU), "Jersey City, Past and Present," Mario Costa, who bought Jersey City's White Mana for $80,000 in 1979 from Webster Bridges (Lou Bridges's brother) explained

Above: White
Mana, Jersey
City. *Photo by M.
Gabriele.*

Right: White
Manna,
Hackensack.
*Photo by M.
Gabriele.*

that the absence of the second *n* dated back to the 1980s. Costa said that the Jersey City diner's sign originally had the spelling as "Manna." He said the sign had been repaired, and when it returned, it was spelled with only one *n* ("Mana"). The misspelling stuck.

Miss America was opened at the corner of Culver and West Side Avenues in 1943. Frederick "Fritz" Welte owned and operated the diner for thirty-five years before retiring in 1978. Born in Germany, he died at age seventy-seven on October 13, 1980, as reported in an obituary by the *Jersey Journal*. Mary Thomas, quoted in the obituary, described Welte as being a good cook and fair boss who was well liked by customers. "He always had a smile and had a charming German accent." Thomas said that she worked as a waitress at Miss America for twenty-two years. The current owner, Christos Stamatis, bought the eatery in 2005.

For Stephanie L. Cherry-Farmer, MHP, senior programs director for Preservation New Jersey, the key word to define the mission of historic preservation is "balance." Formed in 1978 and based in Trenton, Preservation New Jersey is a statewide nonprofit advocacy organization. In 2010, the group listed historic New Jersey diners as among the "most endangered" historic resources in the state. Author Kevin Patrick maintains a website on endangered diners (http://kjpatrick.wordpress.com). "As preservationists, we try to strike a balance and educate people. Historic preservation isn't about freezing time; it's about using the past to build the future. We're guided by long-term stewardship and sustainability. We approach everything on a case-by-case basis," Cherry-Farmer said.

She said that a diner's mobility represents a potential benefit for restoration and relocation, as well as a potential for the loss of a landmark beyond the borders of New Jersey. "Diners are easy to move, but that also means they're easy to move out of the state," Cherry-Farmer pointed out. "We stand to lose them from our own landscape."

A STUDENT OF the Garden State landscape for four decades, architectural historian and author Doug Yorke keeps his eyes peeled for captivating roadside structures. A Jersey guy (he resides in Fair Haven), Yorke was an early observer on the diner scene when, in the March 1977 edition of *Yankee* magazine, he penned "Hash House Greek Spoken Here." In that article, Yorke celebrated the quirky nature of diners. His observations on eccentric ambiance still ring true today:

> *Consistency is not a diner hallmark, but the enjoyment is derived from these differences, for no diner has ever been accused of being monotonous. Each*

diner has its own personal formula, a proportion of these qualities that it has arrived at quite by circumstance. Its personality has been shaped and matured through the years of varying influences, much like any person's might be. Maybe the menu isn't so great, but the grill man sings opera to himself and cracks eggs behind his back. Maybe the tile isn't as clean as it is at home, but the prices are unbelievable and the heap of food just barely fits on the plate. Maybe the waitress is sort of a sloth, but the lemon meringue pie is the sweetest and lightest thing that has ever melted in your mouth.

While he savored the atmospherics, he also raised a red flag. "With the growth of today's highways, the tiny, friendly diners are being shoved aside to make room for the huge, less personal ones. Social progress, in the shape of a bulldozer, is an omnipresent threat." Interviewed in 2013, Yorke lauded Baeder, Cultrera, Garbin and Gutman as being the stalwarts who have fought against this threat. He said they have faithfully documented the "diner phenomenon."

Many diners made a wrong turn during the 1960s and 1970s as they grew larger and took on more "restaurant" characteristics, according to Yorke. The trend was to create space for more tables, but diner counters usually remained the same size or shrank. Tables, he said, became isolated islands of social interaction at the expense of the unrestricted, convivial, free-form dialogue that takes place at the counter between customers, waitresses and proprietors. The result was a more static restaurant environment and less spontaneous diner activity. Yorke also said that lines have blurred during the last thirty years. "The irony is owners of diners have moved away from traditional diner imagery, while at the same time non-diner restaurateurs have adopted the folded, stainless steel look of diners in new retro-style restaurants. What's up with that?"

RANDY GARBIN FEARS that the situation is dire for the survival of vintage, 1950s-era diners during the next five to ten years. He described New Jersey as an especially harsh environment for diner preservation. Part of the dilemma involves stringent government regulations on how and where diners can be moved. He cites a general lack of understanding for a diner's true value and cultural significance in terms of the built landscape of a town or roadway. Often, for a variety of reasons, a municipality simply "wants to get rid of a crusty old diner" in order to accommodate new commercial development, Garbin said. For a township looking to expand its tax base and upgrade its business district, the motives are understandable; from Garbin's perspective, it's a shortsighted approach. In many cases, economic "gravity" dictates the inevitable outcome when a classic diner is on the bubble. An example of one noteworthy diner in danger of going

Elgin Diner, Camden. *Courtesy of James A. McBride.*

to the scrap heap is the Elgin Diner in Camden, a Kullman diner built in the late 1950s that Garbin described as one of most beautiful in the state. As for recent casualties, in early April 2013, Mom's Diner in Avenel, a stainless steel Fodero, was torn down, as reported by Woodbridge Patch.

While cost is always a factor, he said that it takes a special person to successfully relocate and rescue a classic diner. "If you have enough money, you can move anything," he said. "I want people to make as much money as they can, but when it comes to owning a diner, it's more than numbers. You need to have an appreciation for hospitality. You need a gregarious personality, a passion for food and for the atmosphere of a diner." If the primary motivation is simply a return on investment or a fling with nostalgia, Garbin suggested that it's better if the interested party simply "starts from scratch" and invests in a fast-food franchise.

As an artist and historian, Garbin feels a strong bond with the craftsmanship of vintage diners. "They were built beautifully to attract people. These were palaces for the working guy. It's like a grand marquee of an old movie theater. It's designed to make you feel special to be there."

GONE AND NEVER COMING BACK

Classic American Diners, the 2007 book by Don Preziosi, is a pictorial review of his vast diner postcard collection. The images in the tome show the many unique eateries that have been lost over the years. Known as "Diner Don" among his collecting brethren, Preziosi became a full-time postcard dealer in 1980, an occupation he shares with his wife, Newly. He has bought, sold and traded hundreds of postcards over the years, along with other diner-related items such as matchbook covers, ashtrays, photographs, mugs and ephemera.

If arranged in some giant montage, his postcards would form a grand mosaic of a vanishing New Jersey roadside landscape. Taken as a whole, his collection offers a perspective of how widespread diners were in New Jersey. "It's an era in American culture that came and went—that's rapidly fading away," he said. "That would be the story of the [postcard] mosaic. We really are the diner capital, but one by one, the vintage stainless steel diners are disappearing, being bricked over, removed or used for some other type of business."

Max's Grill, the red, barrel-roofed O'Mahony diner located at the corner of Harrison and Manor Avenues in Harrison, built in the mid-1920s, was touted as the oldest diner in the state. In its October 13, 2010 edition, the *Observer*, a weekly Kearny newspaper, carried the headline "Max's Is No More." The diner was demolished in the final days of September to make way for two three-story mixed-use commercial buildings. Max's had been

Max's Grill, Harrison. *Courtesy of Richard J.S. Gutman.*

closed since 2006, according to the article. A story in the *Observer*'s July 21, 2010 edition, with the headline "Goodbye, Old Friend," broke the news that the diner was going to be torn down.

The August 6, 2006 demolition of the Wildwood Diner became a symbol of the seashore resort's vanishing "Doo-Wop" architecture. Located at Spencer and Atlantic Avenues, it was built in 1955 by the Superior Diner Company of Berlin, as mentioned in the book *Doo Wop Motels: Architectural Treasures of the Wildwoods* by Kirk Hastings, who serves as the president of the Wildwood Crest Historical Society. He said that the aquamarine diner was a favorite spot among Philadelphia-area, 1960s rock-and-roll teen idols such as Frankie Avalon, Fabian, Bobby Rydell and Chubby Checker. Hastings said that the diner's demise, which touched a nerve in the community, occurred during a period (2000–2010) when Wildwood lost numerous Doo-Wop structures to condominium development. Doo-Wop is a futuristic, post–World War II design movement known for its flashy neon signs, angular structures, abstract ornamentation and colorful tropical imagery.

Contrasting the loss of the Wildwood Diner, Hastings did note two examples of preservation. The SurfSide Restaurant, built in 1963 and located at Lavender Road and Ocean Avenue in Wildwood Crest, was dismantled in October 2002 and rebuilt to create the Doo-Wop Museum, which opened in 2007. In 2003, Michael John, son of SurfSide owner Tomi John, bought the Crestwood Diner, another Superior eatery. Still standing at Cresse and New Jersey Avenues in Wildwood, the Crestwood was remodeled and renamed the Surfside West diner.

The Lido, a beacon of modern architecture on New Jersey's notorious Route 22 in Springfield, straddled the island median separating the eastbound and westbound lanes of the highway. On July 21, 2003, after fifty-one years of twenty-four-hour service, the Lido closed its doors. The *Star-Ledger*, in its July 22, 2003 edition, ran a four-column photo of the despondent owner John Priovolos—head down, eyes closed, leaning over the counter among stacks of dishes and empty counter stools. Priovolos was quoted as saying that he was in poor health and no longer had the energy to run the diner or the funds to renovate the place. Business, he said, had declined steadily over the years due to the competition—fast-food chains that lined Route 22. Priovolos was unable to find a taker for the Lido, and it was destroyed, replaced by a convenience store. "I couldn't give it away," he lamented to the *Star-Ledger*.

The July 24, 2003 front page of the *Echo Leader* carried a two-column photo of the Lido, with the headline, "A Landmark Disappears." The *Star-*

Ledger story noted that the diner was opened in 1952 by Theodore and Gus Hiotis. The Hiotis brothers previously owned the Lido Food Shop on Thirty-third Street and Eighth Avenue in Manhattan. They borrowed the food shop's name for their new diner, which was built by Paramount in 1960. Prior to the modern Lido, with the signature diamond awning design above its vestibule, there was an earlier Streamline Moderne Lido at the site.

"In Westfield, a Landmark Diner Reluctantly Turns Off Its Grill" was the headline in the *Sunday New York Times'* July 30, 1995 edition. The article referred to the Excellent Diner, a 1947 stainless steel O'Mahony that closed its doors at 2:00 p.m. that day. But the Excellent didn't go to the scrap heap; rather, it was sold to a German businessman who shipped it to Germany. The *Star-Ledger*, in its August 22, 1995 edition, printed a photo of the diner being towed by tractor-trailer truck to Port Elizabeth. The story ("Farewell to Diner; Westfield Eatery Gets New Life in Germany") explained that the Excellent was being transported by container ship to Rotterdam, the Netherlands, eventually to be taken by ferry on the Rhine River to Aalen, Germany. A crowd gathered in downtown Westfield on August 21 to say farewell to the diner. Councilman Norman Greco, quoted in the story, said that he joined the crowd to give the diner "a fond farewell. It was a sad day for Westfield. That was a piece of history that is gone and never coming back."

More than ten years after the diner left town, the *Westfield Leader* in its January 12, 2006 edition reported that the Excellent Diner was serving all-American cuisine to European customers. The diner did land in Aalen, but then it was relocated to a nearby German town named Wasserlassen until it was sold to Disneyland Paris. The Excellent was renamed Café des Cascadeurs ("Café of the Stuntmen") and opened on March 16, 2002.

An August 27, 1995 article in the *Star-Ledger* pointed out that other Jersey diners have been uprooted and shipped to Europe. The Beach Haven Diner went to Barcelona, Spain, in 1992, while Ted's Plaza Diner, Jersey City, near the Holland Tunnel, and the Gateway Diner from Phillipsburg both landed in London. One establishment that made a circuitous route to Europe was the Clarksville Diner, a 1940 Silk City car (originally known as the Princeton Grill) that was located on Route 1 in Lawrenceville. Gutman said that in March 1988, Gordon C. Tindall purchased the Clarksville, which had been slated for demolition, for $3,000 and moved it to Decorah, Iowa. Tindall spent four years restoring the diner and then ran it for five years, until he sold the diner to a television executive from France. The Clarksville left Iowa on October 19, 1998. It returned briefly to New Jersey, passing through the state on its way to Port Elizabeth. The diner was shipped to Antwerp, Belgium, and went to the headquarters of Canal Jimmy in Boulogne-Billancourt, on the western edge of Paris. Gutman said that the diner is not open to the public and is used mainly for private events and receptions.

Part V

The Corridor State

GOING WITH THE FLOW

New Jersey historian John T. Cunningham, in his 1966 book *New Jersey—America's Main Road*, mapped out important trends for the state's growth during the first half of the twentieth century. During the 1920s, "the automobile had begun to take over the pathway between New York and Philadelphia," Cunningham wrote. "New Jersey was being dubbed 'The Corridor State.'" To complement massive infrastructure projects like tunnels and bridges, the Corridor State needed a robust network of interconnected secondary roadways. "Aware that it must improve its internal road system or become a state with fine bridges on either end and chaos in between, the [state] legislature in 1926 set out to spend $300 million for a highway network within the state. New Jersey by the mid-1930s enjoyed a nationwide reputation for its good highways. For more than a century, no state has carried a greater volume of traffic on its transportation arteries, whether that traffic be rail or motor. Truly, New Jersey is America's main road."

According to Cunningham, this complex, sometimes baffling web of roadways provided ready access to the shore, the woods of Sussex County, the farms of Salem and Warren Counties and the country villages of Hunterdon and Morris Counties. These diverse pockets of Garden State life were "not far removed from the nineteenth century," he wrote. It followed suit that motorists navigating the state's macadam trails, eager to visit these unspoiled Jersey destinations, needed staples such as coffee, omelets, hamburgers, home fries and pie à la mode to sustain their journeys.

Throughout the twentieth century, highways and secondary roads in the Corridor State became diner magnets. Bill Leaver, the director of the Paramus Fritz Behnke Historical Museum, said that the diner surge in Bergen County coincided with opening of the George Washington Bridge on October 25, 1931. After World War II, large tracts of farmlands and woodlands were sold and transformed into suburban housing developments. By the late 1950s, Paramus was a haven for shopping malls, which added to the head count of potential diner customers. Leaver cited a list of Paramus-area eateries that included the Clover Diner; Twin Oaks Diner; Valley Diner; Jack's Diner; and Brook's Diner, a favorite truck stop located on Old Route 2 at East Ridgelawn Avenue (Old Route 2 became Route 17 in 1937). The Suburban Diner, which opened in 1956, closed for a major renovation in April 2012 and reopened six months later, according to articles on Northjersey.com and ParamusPatch.com.

George R. Stewart, who in 1953 wrote *U.S. 40: Cross Section of the United States of America*, documented the towns and scenes along the southern New Jersey route and also delved into a highway's metaphysical nature. In doing so, he outlined the home terrain for diners. "A road has been called a 'symbol of flow'—not only of people and things, but also of ideas," Stewart wrote. "We must concern ourselves with the land that lies beside it and the clouds that float above it, and the streams that flow beneath its bridges. We must remember the people who pass along it and those others who passed that way in the former years. We can forget neither the ancient trees that shadow it, nor the roadside weeds that grow upon its shoulders. We must not avert our eyes even from the effluvia of the highway itself. Only by considering it all…shall we come to know, in cross section, the United States of America." Diners are woven into the spiritual tapestry of that panoramic American "cross section" as described by Stewart.

Originally known as the "National Road," Route 40 begins in Atlantic City and runs east–west, cutting through the southern section of the Pine Barrens. Eighty years ago, it stretched continuously more than 3,100 miles to San Francisco (today, the terminus is in Utah). The road opened in 1926 with the start of the numbered federal highway system. The 64-mile stretch of Route 40 that runs through Salem, Gloucester and Atlantic Counties was well stocked with diners. Frank Brusca, a Route 40 aficionado, maintains a website (www.Route40.net) that provides a list of more than thirty-five diners, past and present, found on the Garden

State's portion of the National Road. Today, Route 40 is populated by the Mays Landing Diner, Deepwater Diner, Elmer Diner, Point 40 Diner, Woodstown Diner and others.

In recent years, the romance of Route 40 has been reenergized due the popularity of the HBO TV series *Boardwalk Empire*, a crime drama set in Atlantic City during the Prohibition era, according to Michael Christakos, who, along with his dad, James, owns the Mays Landing Diner, Mays Landing. The diner—a Musi car that was relocated from Clifton (Tick Tock Diner number two)—was opened in January 1995. He said that the diner caters to the transient crowd—tourists from Pennsylvania and Maryland coming in and out of Atlantic City—as well as local customers from towns located along the Great Egg Harbor River.

HIGHWAY 31 REVISITED

During the 1960s, Aglaia Siliverdis worked as an art teacher in the Somerville public school system and enjoyed an occasional lunch at the Tamarack Diner, which was located on East Main Street. She recalled that the diner moved to West Main Street, near the Somerset County Courthouse, and then was eventually closed and was put into storage. Swingle Diners built the Tamarack in 1959, one of the first diners to have a Colonial interior design. The diner's name refers to tamarack wood used for the knee bracing beneath the counter. Tamarack, also known as larch wood, was the material of choice to support the hulls of nineteenth-century whaling ships. Gutman said that this nautical theme carried over into the diner's interior appointments, with ceiling lamps, a wooden ship wheel and interior walls of brick, tile and copper trim—elements to suggest an early colonial inn. "As diner designers looked for new ideas, these Americana diners [like the Tamarack] were seen as a breakthrough," Gutman wrote.

The Tamarack resurfaced in Ringoes on Route 31 (a state highway, formerly known as Route 30 and Route 69), along the southwestern edge of the New Jersey Sourlands. In 1982, Peter Carom, who owned the property on Route 31, took the diner out of storage and moved its three sections (foyer, vestibule and dining area) to the site, opening it as the Amwell Valley Diner.

Simon Siliverdis (Aglaia's husband) and his brothers previously owned diners, and they became intrigued when they learned that Carom was looking to sell the Amwell Valley. "My husband thought it would be fun to

Amwell Valley Diner sign. *Photo by M. Gabriele.*

run the diner for just a few years," Aglaia said with a smile, accenting the phase "for just a few years." They purchased the diner in 1989 and retained its name. Twenty-four years later, Aglaia and Simon are still running the business, along with their son, John. "I had no idea we'd be doing it this long," Aglaia said. "I'm a 'people person,' so I enjoy it. I laugh when I think about how we've almost become like the farmers in this area. We work the same long hours as they do." She and her family will celebrate the silver anniversary of their ownership on April 1, 2014.

The Route 31/Route 202 Flemington Circle was the site of the once-popular Circle Diner. Nicholas Glynos purchased the diner in 1955 and ran it with his brother, James, and brother-in-law, Nick Orginos, for thirty years. Articles in the *Hunterdon County Democrat* tracked milestones in the Circle Diner's evolution. One year after Glynos bought the business, he expanded the diner, doubling its seating capacity to 75 customers. Further expansions occurred in subsequent years, and by 1971, the diner had room to accommodate 240 patrons. An article in the February 13, 1975 edition of the *Democrat* proclaimed that the Circle Diner was "the place" in the area for business people, political gatherings and family dining because of its location at the Flemington Circle.

Glynos sold the eatery in February 1983 and retired. An obituary posted on NJ.com reported that Glynos died on December 6, 2010, in Naples, Florida. He was born on New Year's Eve 1920 in Andros, Greece. He immigrated to the United States in 1947 and opened a restaurant in Jersey City.

On March 3, 1994, the Circle Diner was destroyed in a spectacular blaze. The *Hunterdon County Democrat* reported that the fire was immediately labeled as "suspicious" and that police and state authorities later determined that the eatery had been deliberately torched.

In early April 2013, the Flemington-Raritan Diner was opened just north of the Flemington Circle. In the summer of 2010, NJ.com reported a partnership that owned the Washington Diner in Washington and the Spinning Wheel Diner in Lebanon submitted plans to the Raritan Township Planning Board to build the Flemington-Raritan Diner. Michael Anastasi, a member of the partnership, was quoted as saying that he and his associates planned to run "a traditional diner, a nice little diner."

Traveling thirty miles north on Route 31, past Clinton and over the Musconetcong River, the Royal Diner, a 1950 O'Mahony car, is tucked away in Washington at the corner of Hillcrest Avenue. It originally was known as Hills Diner, established in 1937 by brothers Robert and Wilson "Red" Hill. Wilson Hill ran the diner for forty years and retired in 1978. He died on August 31, 1992, at the age of seventy-seven, as reported in an obituary in the September 3, 1992 edition of the *Star-Gazette*. The eatery changed hands several times until it opened as the Royal Diner in 1990. Just up the road from the Royal Diner, also in Washington, stands the aforementioned Washington Diner, built by Kullman. The diner was renovated eleven years ago.

Farther north on Route 31, a left turn onto Route 46 leads to the Crossroads Diner, located in Belvidere just before the intersection at Route 519. Proprietors Tom and Sandi Zikas celebrated their thirty-fifth anniversary in May 2013, rolling out a vintage menu that included one-dollar hamburgers, a one-dollar platter of eggs, potatoes and toast and coffee for twenty-five cents. Sandi confessed that the anniversary made her feel sentimental when she thought of the decades she has spent with her customers. "Today, we're feeding kids of kids we fed thirty-five years ago," she said. "Families in this area have supported us for years. This is our social life. These are our friends."

The diner was installed at the site in 1956 and enjoys a little-known claim to fame: it's likely the only diner ever built by the Campora Dining Car

Royal Diner, Washington. *Photo by M. Gabriele.*

Crossroads Diner, Belvidere. *Photo by M. Gabriele.*

Company of Kearny. Gutman wrote that Jerry Campora "was the owner of the short-lived company. The company may have built only one diner." If so, then the Crossroads Diner is the one.

In the 1950s, the Crossroads was a stop for passengers on the Greyhound bus line. In the early 1980s, the diner was a favorite spot for young adults on Saturday nights, after closing time at a nearby dance club. "Everyone came here. This is where the real party was," Sandi said. Crossroads today proudly displays its stainless steel exterior, but Sandi said that not long after buying the diner, she and Tom decided to cover the façade with stucco and stone. "The 1950s stainless steel look was out of style in those days," Sandi recalled during a 2012 interview. "But then we realized we didn't like the stucco and stone, so we removed it. Our customers were happy with that decision."

Sandi said that her son, Alex, works as a short-order cook. She praised her husband, Tom, as a dedicated diner man. Prior to buying Crossroads, Tom Zikas worked at the Turnabout Diner, which was located on Memorial Parkway (Route 22) in Phillipsburg. The Turnabout was demolished in late January 1977 and replaced by a Burger King. A photo of the diner's wreckage was published in the January 29, 1977 edition of the *Easton Express*.

MIDDLE-CLASS VALUES

Michael Aaron Rockland (author of the aforementioned October 1977 *New Jersey Monthly* article), PhD, professor of American studies at Rutgers University, New Brunswick, depicted in his 1989 book *Looking for America on the New Jersey Turnpike* (co-written with Angus Kress Gillespie) the 122-mile turnpike, which opened in November 1951, as a symbol of the Corridor State's culture of mobility. "We can appreciate the Turnpike as a living embodiment, a museum really, of the prevailing values of the era in which it was built," the book notes. "This was the era when diners served blue-plate specials, when cars had lots of chrome, and when suburbanites put pink flamingos on their front lawns."

Rockland said that diners are an essential part of New Jersey's "Wheel Estate" and culture of mobility. "The diner is a roadside event. New Jersey is the most densely populated state and a very mobile place. Diners fill an important niche. We have an immense middle class in New Jersey. As Americans, we want to believe we're all middle class. This is the great American myth and it's also the great American ideal. We believe in the equality of opportunity. The diner is a great repository of this ideal. It's the perfect middle-class place to eat.

"For years New Jersey has been the butt of jokes on TV and in the movies," Rockland continued, taking offense at the underlying prejudice that these attitudes convey. "The joke is that New Jersey is mediocre, coarse and unsophisticated. That's the put-down. No, we're not mediocre; we're middle class. We don't take crap from anyone. New Jersey has an authenticity, sincerity and a respectability that people secretly admire. We're for real. This is something to celebrate."

The celebration of these middle-class virtues can even involve spiritual illumination. Fourteen years ago, Reverend Monsignor Francis R. Seymour, KHS, an archivist at Seton Hall University's Walsh Library in South Orange, served as a chaperone for a nineteen-year-old seminarian from Portugal who came to visit the archdiocese of Newark. The two hit it off well, and Monsignor Seymour spent the week escorting the young man to all the familiar tourist sights of New York City. During their time together, the seminarian confessed that he was a fan of American history and culture. Taking the cue, Monsignor Seymour—a Bayonne-bred man of faith and scholarly son of the Garden State sod—asked if there was anything else his young friend wanted to see. The answer was immediate: he wanted to go to a "real American diner," saying that he had heard and read so much about them.

"He said it was the one thing he really wanted to do, more than anything else," Monsignor Seymour recalled. "I guess he was too shy to tell me that in the first place." As a result, the two had lunch at a diner during a road trip to the presidential library and museum of Franklin D. Roosevelt in Hyde Park, New York. Walking through the diner vestibule, the young man was thoroughly captivated. As the two pilgrims sat at the counter, Monsignor Seymour turned to the seminarian, raised his eyebrows, gave a slight tilt to his head and gestured with his open hands as if to say, "So, what you think?" The young man, brimming with joy, answered breathlessly: "It's just like what you see in the movies!"

"I'll never forget the big smile he had," Monsignor Seymour said. "I could see how happy he was. I really didn't have to say much." Having dutifully completed his appointed task, Monsignor Seymour ordered a cup of coffee, sat quietly and recalled the advice of St. Francis of Assisi: preach the gospel; use words only when necessary. Lunch at a diner—a simple, friendly, secular experience—was an epiphany for the teenager during his visit to the United States. He returned to Portugal, continued his studies and became a priest.

Growing up in the "Peninsula City" during the 1940s and 1950s, Monsignor Seymour's favorite place was the Bayonne Diner, a short walk from his home on Fourteenth Street. "A full meal for a dollar, including dessert," he recalled. The downtown diner was closed in April 2009 and then reopened six months later as the Broadway Diner and Bistro. He still visits occasionally, having lunch with Bayonne priests. "We go there because it's convenient and good."

EVERY DAY, DINERS host the ultimate American egalitarian dining experience for saints and sinners. No reservations are required, and none are accepted. There's a stool and a booth for everyone. A diner is the place where wayfarers from any socioeconomic demographic can walk in and grab a bite to eat. Andrew Hurley wrote that diners "challenged Americans from all walks of life to deny the relevance of class…In guiding upwardly mobile Americans into a world of mass consumption, diners encouraged them to adopt new social rituals and new standards for social conduct."

When it comes to adopting standards for social conduct, Rockland readily acknowledges that proper New Jersey diner etiquette is an acquired skill that's handed down from one generation to the next—a street-smart protocol that exemplifies the Garden State's down-home spirit. It includes an appreciation for the subtle, comedic elements that break down artificial class distinctions. "There's a sense of humor to it, but not everyone gets it," he said.

Rockland's correct—not everyone gets it. But then that's half the fun.

Epilogue

In the early 1970s, I was a semi-regular at the Tick Tock Diner, along with my friends Patrick and Bill. Van Morrison's tune "Domino" was our top choice on the jukebox. A late-night breakfast at the Tick Tock really was a "graveyard charade and a late-shift masquerade," as poetically described by the bard Tom Waits. Nick, the avuncular owner, was the star of the show—day or night—encouraging everyone to "eat heavy, my friends" with his gravelly, fatherly voice.

Eat heavy. Aside from the obvious reference to food, it was Nick's way of telling customers to live well, enjoy life, seize the moment and savor the time spent breaking bread together.

Patrick, a most devoted patron, often stopped at the Tick Tock for a second lunch after finishing his classes at Clifton High School. Bill's routine was to sit in a booth and obsessively count half-spoonfuls of sugar in multiples of two for his coffee. I was fond of scarfing up the deep-fried seafood platter and the crullers. Our favorite grill man was George, who frenetically served customers and piled tempting mounds of home fries onto the grill. After finishing our meal, George, speaking with his distinctive Greek accent and smiling nervously, typically had only a few words of advice to bid us farewell as we paid our bill. They were always the same words of advice. "Be good, boys. Don't be hippies," he said each time we stumbled out the door.

As we drove off, with the Tick Tock's silvery reflection growing smaller and dimmer in our rear-view mirror, forty years have flashed by. Today, I live

Photo by M. Gabriele.

less than a mile from the Tick Tock, its blue and red neon lights visible from my backyard. Nice view.

"Domino" on the jukebox, the sizzle of home fries, counting half-spoonfuls of sugar in multiples of two and repeated warnings not to become a hippie. Memories like these are always on the menu. They sustain you, like a prayer.

Eat heavy, my friends. Eat heavy.

Bibliography

BOOKS

Baeder, John. *Diners.* New York: Harry N. Abrams, 1978.

Bellink, Alan, and Donald Kaplan. *Diners of the Northeast.* Stockbridge, MA: Berkshire Traveller Press, 1980.

Cultrera, Larry. *Classic Diners of Massachusetts.* Charleston, SC: The History Press, 2011.

Cunningham, John T. *New Jersey, America's Main Road.* New York: Doubleday, 1966.

Genovese, Peter. *Jersey Diners.* New Brunswick, NJ: Rutgers University Press, 1996.

———. *Roadside New Jersey.* New Brunswick, NJ: Rutgers University Press, 1994.

Gillespie, Angus Kress, and Michael Aaron Rockland. *Looking for America on the New Jersey Turnpike.* New Brunswick, NJ: Rutgers University Press, 1989.

Gutman, Richard J.S. *American Diner.* N.p., 1979.

————. *American Diner, Then and Now.* Baltimore, MD: Johns Hopkins University Press, 1993.

Hastings, Kirk. *Doo Wop Motels: Architectural Treasures of the Wildwoods.* Mechanicsburg, PA: Stackpole Books, 2007.

Heimann, Jim. *Car Hops and Curb Service: A History of American Drive-In Restaurants, 1920–1950.* San Francisco, CA: Chronicle Books, 1996.

Hurley, Andrew. *Diners, Bowling Alleys, and Trailer Parks: Chasing the American Dream in the Postwar Consumer Culture.* New York: Basic Books, 2001.

Marhoefer, Barbara McGeary. *Jerry O'Mahony, Dining Car Pioneer.* N.p.: privately published, 1996.

————. *The Joe Montano Material, His 40-Year Career in the Diner Industry.* N.p.: privately published, 2006.

Martino, Vincent, Jr. *The Wildwoods: 1920–1970.* Postcard History Series. Charleston, SC: Arcadia Publishing, 2007.

Middleton, Kathleen M. *Images of America: Bayonne.* Charleston, SC: Arcadia Publishing, 1995.

Preziosi, Don. *Classic American Diners.* Atglen, PA: Schiffer Publishing Ltd., 2007.

Stewart, George R.. *U.S. 40: Cross Section of the United States of America.* Boston, MA: Riverside Press, Houghton Mifflin Company, 1953.

CITY DIRECTORIES

Bayonne City Directory, 1914–15.

Bloomfield City Directory, 1935 and 1955.

Clifton City Directory, 1952 and 1954.

Jersey City Directory, 1915, 1918 and 1922.

Kearny City Directory, 1915.

Nutley City Directory, various editions.

Union City Directory, 1956.

MAGAZINES

The American Restaurant (December 1921).

Collier's (November 18, 1922).

The Diner (August 1941, February 1941, January 1947, October 1941).

Diner, Drive-In Restaurant (January 1954).

Edible Jersey (Summer 2008).

Fortune (July 1952).

Inside Jersey (August 2013).

Insight (April 9, 2001). Montclair State University.

New Jersey Monthly (February 2013, January 1991, October 1977).

The New Yorker (September 30, 1972).

New York Times Magazine (October 23, 1983).

The Official Gazette of the United States Patent Office (February 7, 1939).

Printers Ink Monthly (June 1922).

Saturday Evening Post (June 19, 1948).

Yankee Magazine (March 1977).

ORGANIZATIONS/OFFICES

Boonton Historical Society, Boonton, New Jersey.

City of Clifton Municipal Assessor's Office, Clifton, New Jersey.

Culinary Arts Museum, Johnson & Wales University, Providence, Rhode Island.

Jersey City Historic Preservation Committee, Jersey City, New Jersey.

Jersey City Landmarks Conservancy, Jersey City, New Jersey.

National Restaurant Association, Washington, D.C.

New Jersey City University, Jersey City, New Jersey.

Office of City of Clifton mayor James Anzaldi.

Passaic County Historical Society, Paterson, New Jersey.

Preservation New Jersey, Trenton, New Jersey.

State Historic Preservation Office/Minnesota Historical Society, St. Paul, Minnesota.

Union Township Building Department, Union, New Jersey.

Wildwood Crest Historical Society, Wildwood Crest, New Jersey.

LIBRARIES AND MUSEUMS

Clifton Main Memorial Library, Clifton, New Jersey.

Dixon Public Library, Dumont, New Jersey.

Easton Area Public Library, Easton, Pennsylvania.

Fritz Behnke Historical Museum, Paramus, New Jersey.

Hightstown Public Library, Hightstown, New Jersey.

Hunterdon County Public Library, Flemington, New Jersey.

Jersey City Free Public Library, Jersey City, New Jersey.

Johnson Public Library, Hackensack, New Jersey.

Kearny Public Library, Kearny, New Jersey.

Middlesex Public Library, Middlesex, New Jersey.

Minnesota Historical Society Library, St. Paul, Minnesota.

Newark Public Library, Newark, New Jersey.

Nutley Historical Society, Nutley, New Jersey.

Nutley Public Library, Nutley, New Jersey.

Phillipsburg Free Public Library, Phillipsburg, New Jersey.

South River Historical and Preservation Society, South River, New Jersey.

South River Public Library, South River, New Jersey.

Springfield Public Library, Springfield, New Jersey.

State Historic Preservation Office/Minnesota Historical Society, St. Paul, Minnesota.

Sussex County Public Library, Newton, New Jersey.

Torrington Historical Society. Torrington, Connecticut.

Torrington Historic Preservation Trust, Torrington, Connecticut.

Washington Historical Society, Washington, New Jersey.

Washington Public Library, Washington, New Jersey.

NEWSPAPERS

Asbury Park Press. September 20, 1959; February 5, 1997; November 15, 2001.

Atlantic Highlands Herald. March 10, 2005.

[Bridgewater] *Courier News.* October 26, 2000.

[Easton, Pennsylvania] *Easton Express.* January 29, 1977.

Elizabeth Daily Journal. May 10, 1956.

[Flemington] *Hunterdon County Democrat.* Numerous articles.

Fort Lauderdale News. June 23, 1981.

[Hackensack] *Record.* Numerous articles.

[Hackettstown] *Star-Gazette.* September 3, 1992.

[Jersey City] *Jersey Journal.* October 13, 1980.

[Kearny] *Observer.* February 24, 1949; October 13, 2010; July 21, 2010.

Newark Evening News. February 3, 1953; November 12, 1961.

[Newark] *Star-Ledger.* Numerous articles.

[Newton] *New Jersey Herald.* November 9, 1972.

New York Times. Numerous articles.

Nutley Sun. August 25, 1977; June 9, 1977; July 7, 1933.

Paterson Evening News. Numerous articles.

[Springfield] *Echo Leader.* July 24, 2003.

[Summit] *Independent Press.* June 22, 1989.

Trenton Times. January 11, 2004.

Union Register. August 18, 1946.

WEBSITES, BLOGS, ONLINE ARTICLES

Cultrera, Larry. "Diner Hotline Weblog." http://dinerhotline.wordpress.com.

Davies' Chuck Wagon Diner. www.davieschuckwagon.com.

Diner Hunter. www.dinerhunter.com.

Flickr. www.flickr.com.

Garbin, Randy. Roadside Online. www.roadsideonline.com.

Mary Corcodilos. Online memoir. www.mastoris.com.

Minnesota Historical Society Library. www.mnhs.org/library.

MLive (Michigan Live). www.mlive.com.

New Jersey Community Development Corporation. "History of Paterson. New Jersey." www.njcdc.org/revitalizing/history-of-paterson.

New Jersey Online. Numerous articles. http://www.nj.com.

Nuvvo. "An Intro to Streamline Moderne." http://art.nuvvo.com/lesson/5937-an-intro-to-streamline-moderne.

Olds, Nancy Jennis. "The Taste of Nostalgia: Visiting 29 Diner in Fairfax." The Connection Newspapers. http://www.connectionnewspapers.com/news/2013/jan/11/taste-nostalgia.

Patrick, Kevin. "Place and Landscape Meaning." http://kjpatrick. wordpress.com.

Printroom. California. www.printroom.com.

Roadside Architecture. http://www.agilitynut.com/roadside.html.

Skee's Diner, Torrington, Connecticut. http://www.skeesdiner.org.

Torrington Historic Preservation Trust, Torrington, Connecticut. http:// www.preservetorrington.org.

Utah Division of State History. http://history.utah.gov.

Wagner, Marc Christian, Preservation Associates of Virginia, Charlottesville. "History." 29Diner website, January 30, 1992. http://www.29diner.com/ history.htm.

Yelp. www.yelp.com.

Miscellaneous

Frank Conte, unpublished memoir, Florham Park, New Jersey.

National Register of Historic Places. National Park Service, United States Department of the Interior.

Index

About the Author

Michael C. Gabriele's first book with The History Press, *The Golden Age of Bicycle Racing in New Jersey*, was published in 2011. A lifelong Garden State resident, he is a 1975 graduate of Montclair State University and has worked as a journalist for more than thirty-five years. He is a member of the executive board of the Nutley Historical Society and serves on the advisory board of the Clifton Arts Center.

Visit us at
www.historypress.net
....
This title is also available as an e-book